STRANGE IRELAND

JACK'S STRANGE TALES BOOK 5

JACK STRANGE

For Cathy

'There's nothing that happens here that isn't strange.'

INTRODUCTION

Once again, it was that most excellent of writers, A. J. Griffith-Jones, who persuaded me to write another Strange book, and for that I thank her. Ireland proved to be fertile ground for tales, beliefs, ghosts, myths, legends and general strangeness.

In this book, I have not differentiated between the two nations of Northern Ireland and the Republic of Ireland. I am not a political writer, nor will I ever be. Where the two countries share similar folklore and history, it would be almost impossible to tell them apart anyway. Ireland is an island of the impossible, with tremendous legends and lore, a history of resistance to invasion and a bitter sense of humour, often directed at herself.

For those who are unsure, Ireland is that island to the west of Great Britain, an island the Romans did not invade and which has a unique culture that has spread around the globe. It is famous for St Patrick's Day, for leprechauns and Guinness, for its friendliness, its saints and its greenness. It should also be famed for its ghosts; for I found so many that I could easily have written a book purely about them. Others have done just that, and far better than I ever could.

This book speaks of ghosts and monsters, of remote islands and airships, of demons and holy men, ancient sights and curses and much more. I have deliberately not included modern politics, or indeed any politics, and I have treated Ireland as a single entity, a unique island on the western fringe of Europe. Although the dominant culture for centuries was Celtic, the Celts were only one People who came to this island. Norsemen from Denmark and Norway, Normans from Wales and England, waves of English, Highland, Hebridean and Lowland Scots have all left their mark on Ireland and have added their quota of strangeness. Yet possibly the Peoples who preceded the Celts gave as much, in an understated, nearly indefinable manner. These people were the objects of many of the stories of the Celts and were possibly the only people in the world of whom the Celts were afraid. They became the fairy folk, the Sidh, and many of them will be encountered in the pages of this book.

This book is split into twenty-six chapters, each one illustrating one particular aspect of Irish strangeness, or one area of Ireland that caught my attention as holding strange stories. The first chapter is a very brief look at Irish history, so the reader can place the occurrences in context. Although the history is as factual as I can make it, in some ways the facts are as strange as any story, legend or myth, and that is the essence of Ireland. Truth and fiction, mythology and legend, overlap, so they become nearly indistinguishable, layer after layer of strangeness interwoven into a Celtic knot of strangeness. Welcome to Ireland.

Jack Strange.

ONE

A BRIEF HISTORY OF IRELAND

IN THE BEGINNING, was the ice, and there was rather a lot of it. When it began to melt away, animals swarmed in, followed, around 8,500 BC, by people. These early Irishmen and Irishwomen were hunter-gatherers, gleaning what they could from the plants and trees, fishing the many rivers and loughs (that's Irish Gaelic for what English speakers call a lake), and hunting the plentiful wildlife. Academics call this period Mesolithic, but we have no means of knowing what these people called themselves if indeed they had any collective nouns to describe who or what they were.

These Mesolithic people roamed around the island, hunting, gathering and producing little copies of themselves for a few thousand years, and then, around 3,500 BC, a fantastic array of now megalithic tombs sprung up across Ireland. The craftsmanship (or craftspersonship if you are politically correct) is as astounding as the astral knowledge. We will meet some of these places later.

These peoples lived in Ireland for another couple of thousand years before the Celts arrived, in approximately

600 BC. The Celts undoubtedly had a significant impact on Ireland, and the language and much of Irish culture, tales, myths and legends come from Celtic roots. When the Romans came to what is now Britain, they overran the island as far as the waist of Scotland, until the Picts repulsed them. Agricola said he could conquer Ireland with a single legion and auxiliaries, but did not have the chance to prove his boast correct. His failure to invade Ireland probably saved the Roman Empire from a great deal of grief, given the difficulties faced by later invaders.

While the Romans eventually brought Christianity to Britannia, Ireland, like Pictland, remained pagan. When the Romans withdrew, and possibly before then, Irish slavers raided Britain. One such raid captured a man that history has made an icon of Irishness; his name has been remembered as Patrick and legend says he was born in Dumbarton, then the capital of Strathclyde. After six years of slavery as a shepherd, Patrick escaped to Continental Europe from where he returned to Britain. According to an Irish poem, St Caranoc baptised him in Candida Casa, now Whithorn, in South West Scotland. Although historians debate the dates, it is likely that he returned to Ireland sometime in the fifth century, possibly in 431 AD. Patrick and his disciples spread Christianity through Ireland, founding a network of monasteries that also served as distribution centres for writing and other civilised culture. Pope Celestine had sent a man named Palladius to Ireland sometime earlier, although his influence seems to have been less than that of Patrick.

With the withdrawal of Rome from Britannia, hordes of Germanic tribes named Saxons, Junes and Angles, invaded their old territories, bringing paganism with them. There was a raid or two from the Anglo-Saxons who had invaded Great Britain, but nothing the Irish could not handle. As Christianity took root, Ireland became a shining light of hope for the western world.

This happy period of growing civilisation lasted until the end of the eighth century when a new force burst into the European theatre, spreading carnage and horror along the seaways and rivers. The Norsemen - or Vikings - had arrived and Ireland would never be the same again. The Norse' first victims were the monasteries, depositories of richly decorated manuscripts as well as of profound knowledge. The pagan Norse destroyed what they could not steal and murdered those they could not enslave. Celtic Christianity wilted under the onslaught. Worse was to come as rather than raiding, the Norse began to settle. Norse colonies sprang up along the coast, forming settlements for trade that in time would become Ireland's major cities. After more than a century of intermittent warfare, the Irish got the Norse under control, and then came the next and even more dangerous invasion.

Ireland was not a single country, but a loose assembly of rival kingdoms, with a High King above all. This High King ruled from Tara, dispensing justice as he tried to establish some sort of order on the unruly sub-kingdoms who theoretically bowed before him. The primary kingdoms were: Munster in the south, Connaught in the west, Leinster in the east, Meath in the centre and Ulster in the north. It was a dynastic dispute in Leinster which led to the next traumatic event in Irish history.

Diarmais Mac Murchada had been king of Leinster until a rival grabbed his throne. Diarmais was aware of the century-old Norman conquest of England and later occupation of much of Wales and asked for Anglo-Norman help to regain his kingship of Leinster. That decision was to prove costly for Ireland and altered the course of Irish history for the next seven hundred years.

The Anglo-Norman lords agreed, with their soldiers defeating the incumbent king of Leinster and placing Diarmais on the throne. Not content with that, the Normans began to attack the other Irish kingdoms. Worse, King Henry II of England supported his knights' interference in Ireland, and the Pope also thought it a good idea. The following year, more Normans invaded Ireland, with Richard de Clare, known as Strongbow, leading them.

Ireland being the strange place it is, the effect of the Norman-English upon Ireland was foretold by a now-unknown scribe.

Wicked is the time which will come then; envy, murder, oppression of the weak, every harm coming swiftly... the hypocrites will come, they will assume the shapes of God – the slippery ones, the robbers.

The Norman- English invaders conquered much of the country, lost some to a counter-attack led by Ruaidri Ua Conchobair, the High King, but retained the main ports and hinterland. In 1171 Henry of England led another Norman-English invasion and grabbed more Irish land. After that disaster, the Norman-English aggression and expansion were met with increasingly bitter Irish resistance. Treaties were made and broken as the Norman-English treated Ireland as if they had a right to own the country and the Catholic Church supported the invaders.

However, although the mailed Normans had an obvious military advantage, the Irish refused to give up. Year after year, decade after decade, Irishman fought the invaders, with gradual success. As in Scotland, the Normans intermarried with the local women, and the children spoke Gaelic and became as Irish as the natives. The Irish slowly rolled the English back until they were enclosed within the 'Pale' – Dublin and the immediate hinterland. Only when the

Tudors were on the English throne was there another concerted English attempt to conquer Ireland.

Henry VIII of England, he of the many wives, self-declared that he was King of Ireland and sent over his armies and the Protestant faith. Decades of fighting saw an English occupation by the end of the sixteenth century. When King James VI of Scotland added England to his thrones, he tried a new tactic to quieten Ireland. He settled Protestants from both Scotland and England in the north of the island, Ulster. King James wished to place a Protestant barrier between Catholic Ireland and the Western Isles of Scotland, from where many thousands of fighting men had sailed to help the Irish in their struggles. A secondary reason was that Ulster had been the part of Ireland most resistant to English control. The native Irish watched the spread of the Scots-English colonists until 1641 when they rose against them in war as bitter as any in history. A Scottish army was sent to Ulster, with mixed fortunes, and later Oliver Cromwell crossed the Irish Sea. By 1652 Cromwell's soldiers had reduced much of Ireland to a smoking ruin and heaped the dead in piles. More land was taken from the Irish and given to Protestant settlers.

As the Protestants tightened their grip on Ireland, new laws struck at the Roman Catholic majority. For instance, Catholics were not allowed to hold public office, follow a professional career or own arms. Despite the repression, the vast bulk of the population remained loyal to the Roman Catholic faith. The island seethed with frustration that occasionally boiled over into risings against the Protestant rulers. Politically, things altered in 1707 when the Scottish and English parliaments merged to form the union known as Great Britain although Ireland had her own parliament, with only Protestants allowed to make the laws.

In 1798, with Europe aflame with the French Revolutionary War, thousands of Irishmen rose against the administration. The British crushed it with some brutality got rid of the Irish parliament and united Ireland with Great Britain. That move was not altogether negative, for in 1829 a Catholic emancipation bill gave more equality to that faith. For centuries, famine had been a constant threat to the largely rural economy of Ireland and in the 1840s a series of bad years helped blight spread across the potato crop, the staple crop of much of the island, particularly in the west. Around a million people died, and another million or so emigrated. Many blamed the British government for the tragedy, intensifying the bitterness already felt. In the 1880s, demand for land reform led to increased violence, and as the nineteenth century ground to its finish and moved into the twentieth, the British government promised Home Rule for Ireland. The First World War intervened, Home Rule was put on the back burner, and Irish anger erupted in the Easter Rising of 1916. To the British authorities, heavily involved in the First World War, this rising was seen as treason, and when the smoke cleared from Dublin, they ordered the execution of the leaders. Ireland watched, seethed and remembered.

Two years later Sinn Fein, 'We Ourselves', the party for Irish independence won the democratic vote and formed a government in Ireland rather than sitting in Westminster. In 1919 the War of Independence began, lasting until 1921. The result was a treaty between Ireland and Great Britain that set up the Irish Free State for most of the island, with the Six Counties of Ulster voting firmly to remain British and forming Northern Ireland. However, there was still no peace as civil war disrupted the new Free State between those who supported the Anglo-Irish Treaty and those who wanted more. In 1949 the Irish Free State declared itself a Republic. The majority of people in Ulster wished to remain British.

Behind the politics, the people struggled on, each intent on his or her own life and worries. And all the time, people lived with their superstitions and strange happenings.

TWO

IN DUBLIN'S STRANGE CITY

'In Dublin's fair city,' the song *Molly Malone* claims, 'the girls are so pretty', and there is no arguing with that fact. Nevertheless, for anybody hunting for a haunting, or anything else strange, Dublin is a greedy city with more than its share of ghosts. The first time I visited Dublin, I did not know what to expect. Perhaps, I thought, a city of slightly faded Georgian elegance with a centre famous for stag parties and pubs. I did not expect such a vibrant, cosmopolitan city with amazing architecture, beautiful parks and open-hearted people. Since that day, many years ago, I have been back many times and used Dublin as my base to explore first the hinterland and then further afield. As the capital of the Republic of Ireland, I think that Dublin is the best place to begin.

It was not until my second or third visit to the city that I began to learn of Dublin's many ghosts. Growing up in Edinburgh, I had come to believe the Scottish capital was the most haunted in Western Europe, but now I would say that Dublin is at least a match. I used my now standard method of educating myself: use published books as a background, consult copies of old newspapers and then visit the localities to taste the atmosphere and, where possible, find the houses and areas supposedly haunted. Finally, when the theories are absorbed, sit in the corner of a local pub, wait until a few obvious regulars enter and ask them if they know about such-and-such a ghost. The results, as always, were fascinating.

Sometimes I was greeted with derision, at which point I thanked my adviser politely and hurriedly left. There is no point in staying where one is not welcome. More often, I was given a garbled account, less concise than I had already learned and one that added nothing to my store of knowledge or details. Occasionally, I met a gem of a Dubliner. Possibly the most significant of these Dublin meetings was when I spoke to a married couple in a pub called Darkey Kelly's. The fact that the pub itself was haunted was not a coincidence, for an Irish friend of mine had happily compiled a list of Dublin pubs reputed to harbour a ghost and recommended which ones to visit.

It was a hard job, touring the pubs in Dublin, but to borrow a well-used cliché, somebody had to do it. Darkey Kelly's is well marked by flags outside and has live entertainment inside, yet my two companions still managed to speak in low voices that conveyed tremendous ghostly atmosphere. That must be an Irish skill. Both asked me not to name them, 'in case somebody ever reads your book and recognises us,' so I have altered the names to Monica and Hugh.

Monica had a knack of widening her eyes when she told me of the darkest parts of her story, which combined with her raven hair and husky voice, added much to her story. She claimed that she was distantly related to the original Darkey Kelly, who was burned for witchcraft, or other offences, back in the bad old days. When I asked if Darkey had really been a witch, Monica touched her hair, made the sign of the Cross and said, in complete innocence. 'Oh, no, she was much worse than that. Darkey was a murderer. Did you not hear about the bodies found right under this building? They were right under where you are sitting, in fact.' I think she was not telling the truth with that statement.

Monica told me that Darkey Kelly was only accused of witchcraft after she said a city official, possibly Sheriff Simon Luttrell, Lord Carhampton, was the father of her child. Luttrell, according to Monica and some other accounts, was a member of the Hellfire Club, a notoriously immoral organisation that flourished in the Dublin area in the eighteenth century. One version of the old tale says that Darkey asked for financial support for her illegitimate child, and in return, Luttrell had her burned as a witch and murdered the child in a satanic ritual.

I had thought the name 'Darkey' related to the colour of her hair, but according to Monica, it was a shortened version of Dorcas. This lady was a Madame who ran a very successful brothel known as the Maiden Tower, in a place, Copper Alley, which branched off Fishamble Street. As Monica said, 'Maiden Tower was a very ironic name for a brothel, but at a time of poverty, Copper Alley is about right for what the girls earned.'

In the dark old days of the seventeenth century, witchcraft was very much frowned on in the British Isles, ever since King James VI of Scotland who later also took over the English throne, had experienced a stormy sea passage that his wife blamed on witches. Indeed, all across Europe, it was open season on witches or anybody who might be a witch, or who looked like a witch, or who was wise in a different manner. By the eighteenth century, the horror had faded away, so it was unlikely that Darkey was executed for witchcraft. More likely is the story that she was executed for murder, with a shoemaker named John Dowling her victim. Darkey killed him on St Patrick's Day 1760 and paid the penalty on the 7th of January, 1761. Her death was gruesome, being hanged and then burned on present-day Baggot Street, once known as Gallows Road.

In the old Irish tradition, her friends held a wake to celebrate her life, but when it escalated into a riot, thirteen of her former companions, prostitutes all, ended up in jail. According to Monica, who knew the legend, the Dublin authorities dug up the ground under the Maiden Tower and found the remains of five men. I never found out if that was another pile of bodies or if Monica was pulling my leg about the dead under my seat. I strongly suspect the latter. Irish people to have a flair for the dramatic and don't seem to allow the truth to spoil a good story.

Darkey's ghost has been seen in the pub, possibly listening to the music or trying to convince the punters that she was never a witch. But Darkey Kelly's ghost also haunts St Audoen's Church, which in itself is worth a visit. The church was built in 1190 and was dedicated to the patron saint of Normandy, which must have rubbed salt into the wounds of the native Irish, still reeling under the impact of the Norman-English invasion.

St Audoen's also has the 'lucky stone' or blessed stone' which is a ninth century grave slab with a now-faintly inscribed cross. Since mediaeval times, people have touched the stone for luck. After a period when it was at Glasnevin Cemetery, the stone was brought back to the church in the latter years of the nineteenth century, and now the Reverent Alexander Leeper guards it against vandalism. Very few visitors see him because he is dead. His ghost is there though, watching.

St Audoen's has steps stretching downward to the sole surviving gatehouse of Dublin's City Wall. Apparently, this gate was known as the Gate of Hell because it opened into an area of Dublin notorious for brothels and other interesting places of nocturnal entertainment. I counted forty steps on the way down and thirty-nine on the way back up, which brings John Buchan's famous book to mind, and on these steps, Darkey Kelly may also be seen, dressed all in green. Halfway down, while looking for her ghost, I heard a slightly different version of her story, for I was told that Darkey was executed for the murder of her unborn child.

I did not see Darkey, but there again; it was raining, so perhaps she was more comfortably ensconced within her nice dry pub, like all sensible ghosts should be.

This whole area of the city is ancient, with charming old streets with a plethora of legends and stories. Another piece of strangeness occurs on the 13th of April, every year when Handel's Messiah is performed in Fishamble Street. Apparently, the Messiah was first played here in 1742, or so the barman told me!

It was Monica who suggested I visit the Brazen Head, a pub which was already on my list. I did not find it a hardship to enter this place, after reading the plaque on the wall that informs the curious that this is Ireland's oldest pub, founded in 1198. In 1895, the *Dublin Evening Telegraph* advertised the Brazen Head as 'The Oldest Established Hotel in the city. It has a frontage like a miniature castle and a strange jumble of rooms inside. In common with many Dublin pubs, the Brazen Head also serves food and hosts traditional Irish music, although I was more surprised to walk in and see Monica sitting at a table, waving to me with a grin on her face.

'I thought I'd see you in here,' she said.

'I did not think I'd see you,' I said.

'I get around in Dub.' Monica looked at me expectantly, forcing me to part with money for a pint.

Although I had read about the Brazen's ghost, it seemed much more real as I sat inside the establishment with Monica telling me the story, complete with facial expressions and words I cannot write down. To Monica, history was not something that happened centuries ago, but something that concerned people as real as herself, and she is not wrong in that.

The ghost in here was a haunt of Bold Robert Emmet, one of the leaders of the 1803 Rising. The United Irishmen used the Brazen as their headquarters, according to Monica, because it was close to Dublin Castle, the seat of British power. Emmet took a room above the door, so he could watch the street for any double agents or known enemies. Emmet did not prove a great leader, and his 1803 Dublin uprising fizzled out in a bit of a riot in Thomas Street, but he was still hanged, drawn and quartered outside nearby St Catherine's Church. Emmet might have escaped the abortive rising if he had not visited his girl, Sarah Curran, rather than running for safety. He was caught, of course, and the visit sealed his place in the nation's gallery of romantic, if unsuccessful heroes. Despite being executed in September 1803, Emmet still pops in for an occasional visit. He can apparently be seen, sitting in a corner, while searching for the hangman who executed him, who was also a customer.

Other famous Irishmen have also frequented this pub, including Michael Collins, a leader of the 1916 Rising. Indeed in 1916 and again during the post-1922 civil war, there was fighting not far from the Brazen Head.

Mention of Robert Emmet brings Kilmainham Gaol to mind. This grim place held prisoners from various risings against the British from 1798 onwards. It closed in 1924, shortly after independence. Not surprisingly, many ghosts remain, particularly in the chapel. In here, in 1916, Joseph Plunkett, a leader of the Easter Rising, had a midnight marriage to Grace Gifford, a few hours before a firing squad made her a widow. Plunkett's final words to her were said to be: 'Goodbye, darling wife. In another and far happier life, we shall meet again.' Gifford was only three hours married when her man was executed. Her sister, Muriel, was married to Thomas Macdonagh, another leader of the same rising, whom the British also executed.

When the jail was being restored in the 1960s, the workmen reported all sorts of strange activity. Footsteps behind them when nobody was there, lights flicking off and on, stray gusts of wind buffeting them as they worked on scaffolding and up ladders.

Another place Monica recommended was John Kavanagh's, also known as the Gravediggers. Beautifully situated next door to Glasnevin cemetery, this pub opened in 1833. It is a place of myths, with stories that insist there was once a hatch between the pub and the graveyard, so thirsty gravediggers could come for a fly pint. Apparently, that never happened, although there was an arrangement whereby gravediggers could get drinks through the cemetery railings. There is also a ghost, of course, a well-dressed man with a winged collar and pince-nez spectacles. He sits at the back of the bar. Others claim that the spirit is dressed in tweeds while Monica told me that she does not talk to him because he never buys a round. We will return to this area, although not this pub, in the next chapter.

Another fascinating haunted pub is the Lower Deck, a cable's length from Dublin Canal in Portobello Harbour and frequented by locals, which is always a good sign for a decent pint. Sometime in the nineteenth century, a lock keeper on the canal made a serious error and sunk a barge, with the deaths of the crew. His later death, not long after, was possibly connected. The lock keeper hangs about the pub, perhaps pondering his actions. Once again, I did not see him. For a man who seeks out the strange, I am singularly unfortunate in my sightings of ghosts. Nevertheless, I continued my pursuit, following an erratic trail of haunted hostelries across the city.

A pub with a story and strangeness is Mulligans, which has served drinks to the thirsty since 1782, if not always on the same site. Mulligans is arguably the most famous pub in Dublin, frequented by the great, the literary great, local students, those who seek a good pint and my good self. It is in the strangely named Poolbeg Street, a seemingly old-fashioned establishment with the aura of the past only enhancing the ambience of the present. Originally on Thomas Street, Mulligans flitted a few times before ending up where the pub is today. It has been standing here since 1854, the year that the Crimean War began and the Royal Irish Hussars won deathless fame at the Charge of the Light Brigade.

Among the famous people who were said to have watered here is one John F. Kennedy, once President of the United States, the television presenter Eamonn Andrews and the racehorse owner with the splendid name, Mincemeat Joe Griffin. Some people have never left, such as the American who is inside the clock, or rather his ashes are. Now that is strange. According to legend, the barmen have seen ghosts here, although when I made enquiries, the rather large fellow I asked denied all personal knowledge of things supernatural. 'The only spirits here are in the bottles,' he told me, straight-faced. He might have been pulling my leg, of course.

I did hear about the Garda's raid sometime in the 1960s

when the authorities were concerned that Mulligan's was becoming too convivial at a time when the good people of Dublin should be quietly in bed. In smart uniforms and hard of heart, they knocked politely on the door like the crack of doom. At that time, the barman was one Thomas McDonnell, more commonly called Briscoe and he ushered his clientele into the cellar before allowing in the police. When the *Garda* entered, they found a respectably empty pub, had a look around and left. If they had gone upstairs, they would have seen the Abbot of Kilnacrott Abbey, happy with a bottle of claret.

Although the barman I spoke to disclaimed all knowledge of ghosts, there are tales of mysterious footsteps and a ghost who sits on a barrel in the cellar. Somewhat reluctantly, I thought, he revealed that a previous barman saw a bottle of brandy fall or rise from a shelf of its own accord, while sometimes footsteps are heard where there are no people around. 'But I never heard them myself,' he added.

It was hard to tear myself away from Dublin's convivial public houses, but once outside, easy to explore what is undoubtedly one of the most storied and exciting capital cities in Europe, with a plethora of ghost and ghost related stories.

Sometimes the ghosts are not all they are meant to be, such as the incident that came to court in Dublin in February 1885. A solicitor's clerk named Anthony Waldron claimed that his next-door neighbours, Patrick Kiernan and his family, had been banging on his door and throwing stones at his window since 1881. Waldron took Kiernan, the mate of a merchant ship, to court to claim £500 damages to repair his house.

Kiernan indignantly refuted the charges. Frowning to the court, he said that Waldron's house was undoubtedly haunted, and rather than himself or his innocent family, some malignant ghost or spirit had damaged Waldron's house. Or perhaps a lodger or other in Waldron's house had caused the trouble. When Mrs Waldron was called to give evidence, she muddied the waters and maybe damaged her husband's cause when she claimed to see a hand with a diamond cutting one of the panes of glass in her window. Mrs Waldron lifted a billhook (every house should have one handy) and hacked at the hand, chopping off a finger. However, when she later looked, there was neither a finger nor any blood. Waldron must have wondered whose side his wife was on.

Mrs Waldron also said that one of her maidservants had been frightened by strange noises, tripped, fell and spilt a pail of water over herself. Reading the court case, even after the passage of years, it is easy to see Kiernan's expression of, 'I told you so!' The case for the spirit world seemed to be nearly proven until a policeman gave his evidence. He had seen another of Waldron's servants hammering at the door with her heels at the same time as Waldron heard the knocking. Without investigating the case further, the court found in Kiernan's favour. The moral of this strange case is – don't put your hand through the window of a Dublin housewife if you wish to keep all your fingers.

Around the 1880s and 1890s, a new interest in ghosts and things supernatural seemed to spread through Ireland. Ghost stories became popular, and many people began to see or at least believe in ghosts again, or perhaps admit their long-held superstition. With its long and often disturbed history, Dublin was a natural haven for such beliefs, and the ancient Christ Church Cathedral became the focal point for hopeful ghost hunters. For some unexplained reason, the native Dubliners believed that the monks, who used to inhabit the Cathedral, had returned after a thousand years and would relive – if that is the correct term - their old ceremonies. By August 1890, great crowds gathered night after night in the cathedral precincts to witness this event, and night after night they were disappointed. Some only remained a few moments while others stayed through the hours of darkness nearly until dawn. It was weeks before that trend faded, with nobody ever seeing a single monk. The disappointment must have turned men to drink.

The 1890s saw other spiritual manifestations in Dublin, such as the Georgian House in Duke Street, where an old man lay dying in his bed. As he faded away, all the door-knockers began to sound, with the house-bells, used to summon the servants, joining in the din as if calling the dying man to heaven. Instead, the spirit of a young female, known as Kitty, appeared, said nothing and disappeared through a closed window. A lady in that same house, years later, heard the voice of her long-dead great aunt calling her, and she and her aunt fled to the street outside. That house had long been haunted, with ghosts or something in one of the upper rooms enjoying teasing the maids by turning the bed to face in different directions and ripping off the bedclothes, irrespective of who happened to be sleeping in it at the time. Naturally, for everyone who believed in ghosts, there were a dozen who scoffed at the very idea. Two of the latter, brash young men with a high opinion of themselves and no belief in the supernatural, decided to dare the spirits and sleep in the haunted room. The usual inhabitants of the house wished them all the luck in the world and watched them swagger up to bed. Next morning both young men were in the drawing room, one white-faced and shaking, the other sleeping. Neither gave a full account of what had happened, but they agreed that something had that thrown them out of bed and they vowed never to return to that room.

Many other houses seem to have been infested around this time. For example, there was a house in Clarendon Street, which malevolent spirits disliked. Every so often in the 1870s, something outside would throw volleys of stones against the walls, breaking the windows and terrorising the people inside. If that happened once, the police would have probably blamed mischievous boys, but it became such a regular occurrence that crowds gathered to watch the spectacle. Some actually saw the stones lifted from the ground and thrown at the windows, which is strange for any ghostly event.

It seems that, shortly before the stone-throwing began, a man had died inside the house, so people put two and two together and came up with a ghost. They may well have been right.

As is common with most ghost stories, the majority of Dublin's ghosts lack detail. There is only the bare outline of a story with no proper explanation. For example, a house in the elegant Grafton Street has a ghost with a white face and a red beard. Who he is and why he is haunting the place is not known. Whitworth Road in the 1920s had a house where the ghost only appeared one night a year, the anniversary of a nineteenth-century murder. On that night the horrified inhabitants were treated to a re-enactment of the crime, complete with screams and blood. About the same time, a house in Haddington Road was infested with what was termed a 'vapoury luminous globe' that roamed around a room for a while and then vanishing into nothing.

There is slightly more detail about a ghost in Kingstown who appeared in the ghost-heavy 1880s. A man named John Comerford rented a house in Kingstown on a short, six-month lease in 1887 but left after only a few weeks, claiming that the house was haunted. When the landlord took Comerford to court, he told the hearing that his wife had seen 'a young woman with her sleeves tucked up, walking about the bedroom at night.' The ghostly woman also had a 'halo of light around her head.' Seeing the ghost once was bad enough, but when it became a regular occurrence, Mrs Comerford refused to remain in the house any longer. When she spread the news about the ghost, the landlord said it was now hard to rent the house. Taking pity on the man, the court ordered the Comerfords should pay three months' rent.

A decade later, in 1896, Dublin buzzed with rumours about a ghost in upmarket Merrion Square. An unnamed couple, husband and wife, were tenants of a house in that locality, with the husband seriously ill. Indeed, he was so severely ill that everybody expected him to die at any time and his wife bought herself a full collection of black mourning clothes during a summer sale. Still clinging to life, her husband discovered what his wife had purchased and was most upset. Rather than praise his wife for her thrifty forethought, he ordered her out of his house. Now it was the woman's turn to be upset. Rather than leave the house, the poor wife took an overdose of something nasty and died. When her funeral was announced, her brother arrived and met her coming down the stairs.

'I thought you were dead,' he said.

When she continued to walk downstairs, not saying a word, the brother realised that he was trying to talk to a ghost. He met her a second time, and a third, until he became quite used to seeing his dead sister on the stairs of the house. As he prepared for her funeral, his brother-in-law, also died, far too late to be convenient.

With no living tenants, the house was re-let, with Lord and Lady Ashbourne taking over the lease. Both of them saw the ghost on the stairs, sometimes wearing her infamous black mourning dress and sometimes in white. After a while, with the spirit gliding past them nearly every time they used the stairs, they also left the house. Now that's a strange little story.

Another of Dublin's most attractive areas is St Stephen's Green, said to be home to several ghosts. It is the home of the Shelbourne Hotel, built in 1824 and with an impressive 255 rooms. Before the hotel was built, a row of houses stood here and here, in 1791, a young girl named Mary Masters died of cholera. Others put the date of her death as 1846, but either way, she haunts the corridors, rooms and basement of the hotel, slamming doors and turning on taps.

Michelle Obama, JFK and the Rolling Stones have all stayed in this hotel. Lily Collins, actress and daughter of Phil Collins, spoke of seeing the ghost when on the US talk show 'late night with Jimmy Fallon.' When guests complained that one room was haunted, a member of staff was ordered to sleep in the room to see if anything happened. Apparently, she saw taps turning on and off and came out shaken.

Another spirit around here, and arguably the strangest, is also one I found little about. Apparently somewhere around here is the ghost of a seven-foot one-inch British army officer who was active during the rising of 1798. That was a bad time when many Irish rose against British rule and the Republican French sent over a few thousand men to further the trouble. Still scared after the recent Royal Navy mutinies and fearing the French could invade Britain by the back door, the British responded to the rising with sickening brutality. One of the officers, who helped terrorise the population, was the seven-foot giant who still haunts St Stephen's Green. According to the apocryphal legend, he fastened a noose around the necks of captured patriots (or rebels, if you prefer) and hanged them from his own shoulder.

From the same eighteenth century came the Hellfire Club, an organisation which I first met when I wrote a book about the strange goings-on in England. The English Hellfire Club was the original, as early as 1719, and soon after the bucks of Dublin created their own. Even if a tenth of the legends were true, the Irish Hellfire Club would be a place to spawn a hundred ghosts. Drinking, fornicating, gambling, bear and bull baiting were all expected from the upper classes at the time, but the Hellfire Club went further with their worshipping of Satan – allegedly.

The early Hellfire Club under Richard Parsons, Earl of Rosse and Grandmaster of the Freemasons, and including Sheriff Simon Luttrell of Darkey Kelly infamy, drank, debauched with prostitutes and gambled. Indeed, Luttrell gambled so heavily he got himself into serious debt and allegedly sold his soul to the devil to get out. That may be why he was known as the King of Hell.

In time the Hellfire Club shifted home to Montpelier Hill in the Dublin Mountains, where William Conolly had built his hunting lodge from the stones of a Bronze Age tomb. I have given that place a chapter all of its own, later in this book.

In late 1896, it was St Patrick's Cathedral that temporarily became the centre of the Dublin ghost-hunter's world. The choir was in regular practice for Christmas when one of the female members and 'a lady well-known in Dublin society' according to the press, saw the hazy shape of a man sitting in one of the stalls. As she looked, the haze cleared, and the man became more distinct. He was sitting down, paying rapt attention to everything that the choir was doing. The woman gave a gasp of surprise that spoiled the regularity of choir practice and caused the other members to frown at her with intense disapproval. She apologised without immediately giving any reason for her lapse until later that evening, when she told her husband. The man who had been watching had died years ago. He had been one of the clergy of the Cathedral.

Nevertheless, when the husband made tentative enquiries, other people spoke out, mainly Cathedral staff who admitted they had also seen the deceased gentleman, whose spirit inhabited the Lady Chapel of the Cathedral. That place had been of immense interest to the man when in life, as he was in the habit of holding services, particularly for the local poor. The man had loved St Patrick's, often played the organ until the wee small hours and was in the habit of climbing to the top of the tower to make astronomical observations. He was also known to have believed in spiritual activity, which increased the idea that he had returned to the place he deeply loved. Interestingly, he had lived in an ancient house very near the Cathedral, and convinced himself and others that it was haunted, having heard noises very like somebody 'shuffling his feet along the floor' in an upper room, although nobody could be seen. Because the room was used as a library, people thought some unfortunate person had been locked in, and checked the room thoroughly, to find it empty.

As news of the ghost spread around the city, people flocked to St Patrick's Cathedral in the hope of seeing the spirit. So much that public access was restricted for a while. Perhaps the surge in publicity scared the ghost away, for he vanished. He may still be there, sitting in the shadows, enjoying the ambience of a place he still loves.

Headless horsemen are known in many countries, but a headless horse is rarer, so trust Dublin to have six at once. These headless horses appear around Old Bawn Road and the Dodder on the 8th of September, with the coach they pull having two mysterious passengers and a pair of footmen. One of the passengers is said to be Archdeacon Bulkeley, although another version of the legend claims that Bulkeley is driving the coach.

Archdeacon William Bulkeley undoubtedly had local connections as he built the impressive Old Bawn House in this area in 1635. He was the son of Lancelot Bulkeley, the Archbishop of Dublin, who tried to stop Roman Catholics holding masses in public and was stoned for his pains. Trouble seemed to follow the family, for Old Bawn House was hardly completed when the Rising of 1641 broke out, and the house was targeted and suffered much damage. It has now been demolished, but the memory remains in the shape of the ghosts. However, it is not wise to look for the Archdeacon's coach, for according to the legend, anybody who sights it will die within a year and a day. I would avoid the area on the 8th of September, which is the anniversary of the date of the Archdeacon's death, when the coach clatters up to Old Bawn House, which, incidentally, was home to the first Irish stud.

From Old Bawn Road I decided to move to more open spaces, and where better than Phoenix Park?

It is impossible to visit Dublin without seeing Phoenix Park, once a royal hunting park and open to the public since 1747. With a history of military manoeuvres and visits by significant figures, it is now Dublin's main recreational centre and lung. Phoenix Park is undoubtedly one of the most historic parks in Europe. Within the park, in Chesterfield Avenue, named after a former Lord Lieutenant of Ireland, is Aras an Uachtarain, once the Viceregal Lodge and now the official residence of the President of Ireland. Not surprisingly, it is also haunted.

One of the ghosts is Sir Winston Churchill, one-time

Prime Minister of the United Kingdom and a man reputed to have offered Ulster to Eire in return for the wartime use of the latter nation's ports against Hitler's Germany. Churchill's ghost was seen in the house one Christmas in the early 1970s when de Valera was President. Although the mansion is an official residence, it is also a family home, and de Valera's family were gathered for Christmas. The children were playing a game that included a lot of running and shouting, as is right and proper for little people, when three of the President's grandchildren ran into a quiet, barely used part of the house. Chased by a larger group, the three ran into a dark corridor where they saw a strange little boy in clothes that even they recognised as being out of date.

The three children felt a sudden drop in temperature and knew that something was far wrong. The strange boy's face was vaguely familiar at first, and then the children realised that he was a much younger Winston Churchill, whose portrait graced one of the walls in the house. Even as they stared, the image slowly dissipated, and the boy was gone. Naturally afraid, the three children ran back to the adults to report what they had seen.

By that year, Churchill was gone, but as a child, he had known the mansion well. He lived nearly next door in what was then the Little Lodge when his father was secretary to the then Viceroy, the Duke of Marlborough.

The environs of Dublin seem to be as haunted as the city itself. This is the area where once stood the Paling, the divide between the 'safe' or English controlled lands of Dublin and the outer territories of the 'Wild Irish.' To go 'beyond the pale' was to risk all sorts of danger and death. These pleasant lands were once dotted with the mansions of the wealthy, many of which had their own strange tales attached.

In one of these houses, Newlands House, towards the

end of the nineteenth century, new tenants named Charles, and Louisa Andrews arrived. The house was an impressive Georgian building, nine bays long and two storeys high. It had been empty for some time and had a reputation for strange goings-on, although nothing sinister had been reported. For the first few weeks, nothing untoward happened, and the new couple began to relax into their home. On the third Saturday, after they arrived, Charles Andrews had to travel into Dublin on business, leaving Louisa alone in the house apart from her servants. As he was expected back the same night, Louisa waited up for her husband, sitting in her chair or pacing the dining room floor. Downstairs in his parlour, the aged butler also waited for the return of his master.

The clock struck half-past eleven, and no sign. Quarter to twelve and there was still no sign of the master of the house. The minute hand jerked toward midnight, and both the butler and Louisa Andrews heard the sound of wheels on the gravel drive, accompanied by the drumming of horses' hooves. 'At last,' Louisa rose from her chair and moved towards the door, knowing that the butler would be there first. She heard the carriage turn into the avenue leading to the house, and the increasingly heavy hammer of hooves as the iron-rimmed wheels ground on the gravel. Louisa frowned, why was Charles driving the horses so fast? He was usually a staid, sensible man, and their brougham was not quite a speedster.

Slightly concerned but not yet worried, Louisa stepped downstairs to see the butler already opening the front door. His rheumy old hands found the bolts stiff so he moved very slowly. Louisa was growing impatient before the door finally creaked open.

'Thank you,' Louisa said, stepping outside, expecting to

see Charles hurrying to meet her. He was not there, and neither was the coach. The driveway was empty, and a three-quarters moon ghosted pale light over the deserted grounds. It was impossible for a coach and horses to disappear in such a short space of time, so Louisa and the butler stared at each other in consternation. When the full implications stuck them, confusion altered to alarm. Hurriedly closing the door, they nearly ran back to the drawing room, shut the door and sought the comfort of the fire as they discussed what they had just experienced. They had both distinctly heard a coach and horses, yet when they opened the door, there had been none. Both were convinced they must have heard a ghost.

An hour or so later, Charles returned home from Dublin to find Louisa pale-faced, trembling and in a state of shock, with the butler in an even worse state. Within a few weeks, the butler died; the shock had been too much for him. Naturally, Charles made a few local enquiries, asking if anybody had been fooling about with a coach near his house. The answers possibly surprised him.

Nobody had been fooling about with a coach and horses near Newlands House, but many people thought they knew what had happened that night. Away back at the beginning of the nineteenth century Arthur Wolfe, First Viscount Kilwarden had owned Newlands. Wolfe had been an important man in his time, being born to wealth as the grandson of William Philpot, a successful Dublin merchant. Trinity College educated, Arthur Wolfe was a successful lawyer and a member of a high-profile family, with his brother Peter as High Sheriff of Kildare. MP for Coleraine and then Jamestown, Arthur Wolfe was also Solicitor General for Ireland, reputedly a stickler for the letter of the law. As such he clashed with many of the Protestant Ascendancy, of which he was a member. This is no place to enter into the tangle of legal politicking of the era, but Wolfe seems to have tried to be a decent man in difficult times, although in 1797 he succeeded in prosecuting William Orr, a United Irishman, on slender evidence. Orr's subsequent execution left a stain on Wolfe's life and made him an object of vituperation among the United Irishmen.

In July 1798, Arthur Wolfe became Baron Kilwarden and made an abortive attempt to warn the Irish patriot and his relative, Wolfe Tone, to leave the country. As Viscount Kilwarden, Arthur Wolfe supported the Irish-British Union of 1801. Two years later, Ireland was aflame in what has been called a rebellion, but may also be termed a patriotic rising.

With the United Irishman still seething over the execution of William Orr, Arthur Wolfe's life was in danger. On the 23rd of July, as a body of rebels – or patriots – were approaching, he took his nephew the Reverend Richard Wolfe and his daughter Elizabeth and fled from Newlands House. He ordered the coach driver to go through the centre of Dublin rather than by the quiet by-ways, but in Thomas Street, a horde of rebels blocked his coach. When they demanded to know who he was, Arthur Wolfe told the truth, and, according to some versions, the insurgents said 'you're the one we want,' promptly hauled him outside and pierced him with their pikes, doing the same to the Reverend. Elizabeth was unharmed and ran to the authorities in Dublin castle.

As the military cleared Thomas Street, Arthur Wolfe was still alive but died not long after. All well and good, one may ask, but what has that to do with an invisible carriage? According to one version of the story, after the attack on Wolfe, the four horses of his coach ran amuck, hauling the coach, spattered with the blood of its owner, right to the doors of Newlands House. Every so often, history repeats itself, and the sound of the coach and horses has been clearly heard by people inside the house. When I asked about the house, I was told it was knocked down in the 1980s, and the site was now a car park. Perhaps the sound of the internal combustion engine will drown out any clattering of horses' hooves.

From Newlands, we'll scurry to Monkstown and the Widow Gamble.

Once known as Carrickbrennan, Monkstown is now a south Dublin suburb and a pleasant spot to visit, and probably in which to live. From the middle ages to the sixteenth century Reformation, there was a monastery here, with the monks doing whatever monks do as they followed a consistent pattern of life for centuries. The monks, along with the monastery, are long gone, but there is at least one survivor from the past in the shape of Widow Gamble, who may also be called the Widow Gammon.

The Reformation hit Ireland hard, as the now-Protestant establishment persecuted the holy men of the Catholic majority of the population. If it was bad in the sixteenth century, it became worse in the seventeenth when Oliver Cromwell brought his own brand of religious austerity to a reluctant, seething Ireland. With Cromwell's Roundheads hunting zealously for them, the monks scattered, to hide in various places, from special rooms in grand houses to barns and stables.

Not everyone supported the monks, with those locals who followed the Protestant faith, passively and sometimes actively supporting Cromwell. Among the latter was one woman who has come down in folklore as Widow Gamble. According to legend, this unsavoury woman told Cromwell's men where a bunch of Catholic monks were hiding, with the result that the soldiers dragged out the unhappy holy men and executed them. The Widow pocketed her silver as a reward.

Naturally, the area is now haunted. Not by the monks, but by the widow. Apparently, her ghost can sometimes be seen where the soldiers grabbed the monks. If you happen to see her, you're advised to keep your distance, for when one man came close, the widow took hold of his neck, leaving a burn that lasted for the remainder of his life. Such a power would suggest that the Widow is rather more malignant than a mere ghost.

Apart from the unpleasant spirit, there are other reminders of the Widow. There is a house named Gamble's Lodge, a bar called Widow Gambol's and crossroads known locally as Gamble's Hill. Folklore apart, did this nasty woman really exist? Apart from the story I have already related, there are others. As well as pointing out priests to their persecutors, she was also said to be a demi-witch who begged for charity and cursed those who refused her. The two are not mutually opposed.

The Widow's death is also disputed. While some accounts claim a mob hanged her for betraying the monks, others are sure that she cursed a child to give it a pig's face, so the child's father poisoned her.

Whatever the truth, there is no doubt that the Widow's ghost is said to haunt various places in Monkstown. The most popular seems to be Carrickbrennan Graveyard, where she can be seen carrying a key and an axe, although I am not sure what the symbolism implies. According to local historians, the Widow might have been a certain Englishwoman named Hannah Gamble who kept the Sign of the Ship Inn at Blackrock, not far away, but in the eighteenth century, so a century after Cromwell's men had gone. When her husband died, the Sign of the Ship earned a new name of Widow Gamble's.

And here comes another of these strange coincidences that seem to bedevil Irish legends.

As well as Widow Gamble, there was a Widow Gammon, who lived in the nineteenth century and made a living as a vintner, so it is possible that the names have become confused over time.

The Widow will never be lonely in Monkstown, for there are other spirits around Mounttown Hill. There are the usual fairies, a headless horseman and a tendency for horses to refuse the climb the hill.

With the confused tale of the widow, or widows, I shall wave a fond farewell to that aspect of Dublin, but we'll be back. Anyway, I'm not moving far away.

THREE

STEALING THE DEAD

Until recently, people believed that on Resurrection Day, the dead would be brought back to life in the same state as they died, so if they were missing an arm in life, they would be the same in death. Given that belief, it is not surprising that teachers of anatomy, who publicly dissected human bodies to teach their students, were distrusted. Anatomists needed a constant stream of fresh dead bodies, which hanging judges tried their best to satisfy, but when demand outran supply, it was the time of the sack-'em-up-men, the body snatchers or resurrection men.

These gentlemen haunted graveyards for recently buried bodies, sneaked in at night time, dug them up and sold them to the anatomists. They had to take care not to be seen by the night watchmen, who would give no mercy to any grave robbers they found, so the body snatchers became expert at the job, with a recognised procedure. After bribing the church caretaker, or ensuring that he and the watchmen were absent, the resurrection men chose their grave. They carried a sheet to place on the ground to catch the dirt, a short, sharp wooden tool for digging, as metal spades made too much noise, a large sack or two and two irons hooks attached to lengths of rope.

The technique was simple; dig a hole at the head of the coffin, drop the hooks so they attach to the lid and jerk quickly upwards with the idea that a section of the coffin would break off. If the graverobbers were lucky and nobody heard the sound, they could reach down and drag up the body inside. The next step was to remove the grave shroud, or whatever the body was wearing, and return that to the coffin. Stealing clothes was a criminal offence. Now all that remained was to pack the naked body inside the sack, escape with the plunder and find an anatomist with a shortage of teaching material.

Although any graveyard in the country was vulnerable to attack, some became notorious for the number of times they were robbed. Kilgobbin Churchyard at the strangely named village of Stepaside and the equally beautifully named Bully's Acre near Kilmainham, south Dublin seem to have been prime targets. The other name for this latter graveyard was Hospital Fields, which does nothing to enhance the reputation of medical professionals. The gravediggers had to be careful here, for the Royal Hospital often had soldiers as guests, and they would be very unhappy if somebody stole any of their colleagues who were buried in Bully's Acre. The Royal Hospital had its own strangeness, of course, with a Colonel Venner, in the early eighteenth century, having a pet fly that perched on his shoulder. The veteran soldiers in the hospital used to patrol the graveyard for illegal burials, riots and grave robbers.

Glasnevin was another favoured spot. Indeed, in one incident in early 1830, a gang of gravediggers clashed with men mourning a recent burial and there was a gun battle over the graves. A gentleman named Edward Barrett was buried in the churchyard on Wednesday 27th of January, 1830, but as there were fears that the 'sack-'em-up' men might wish to dig him up, a party of watchmen stood guard. On a snowy Saturday the 30th of January, a resurrection gang appeared, only to run when the watchmen challenged them. They gathered reinforcements and returned shortly after two o' clock on Tuesday morning. The six watchmen saw four men standing on the churchyard wall with others trying to climb up beside them. The watchmen shouted at them to get away, only for the resurrection men to fire a volley at them with pistols and muskets. Never men to run from a battle, the watchmen fired back, so the gunshots echoed across the graveyard with the sack-'em-up men hiding behind the churchyard wall and the watchmen sheltering behind the tombstones. At least one of the resurrection men was shot, and the quantity of blood suggested others were also hit.

The battle continued for about fifteen minutes, during which time one of the watchmen rang the church bell to summon help. Townsfolk in their nightshirts and the parish constables ran to help, and the attackers melted away.

Five years later, in July 1835, two opposing parties clashed with stones being thrown and the wooden palings around the graveyard torn down and used as weapons. According to newspaper reports, the rival gangs were the Donnybrook Boys and the Dublin Defenders. In September of that same year, William Walker, the sexton, was attacked by a group of men during a funeral service. As the group were kicking Walker, somebody shouted, 'don't beat him on consecrated ground,' so the men carried him outside the cemetery and continued the assault until the Reverent Kelly stopped his funeral service to save the sexton.

The army was called in to keep the peace, with horse and foot patrolling the area.

Riots seemed to be normal at Glasnevin, with another in 1837, during and after a funeral. Around a hundred men are said to have taken part, with 'men knocked down in all directions' according to the press, and names such as Peter-the-Gatch and Paddy-go-Mad and Ragged Paddy involved as they tried to stop the funeral coach. The coachman responded with his whip. The fight seemed to be between two rival parties, the St Patrick's Society and the society of Billy Welters, who the St Patricks' considered a 'robbing, murdering and plundering set'.

There was a second funeral at the same time, and the fight halted to ensure they did not run over the coffin of an innocent young girl and then started again. Strange goings-on at Glasnevin!

Glasnevin is a vast place at 124 acres and now holds a million bodies. I visited when I was in Dublin, and if the time of my visit was typical, it serves as a place of family gatherings as well as internments. I have looked at a variety of graveyards in many cities in my researches, but only Glasnevin had a watchtower that could be moved from place to place to guard against thieves. The other methods, such as mort stones, mort cages and laying layers of branches over the graves to make digging up the graves harder, would also be used.

As well as the watchtowers, Glasnevin had bloodhounds, with one local telling me they were kept deliberately hungry so they would tear any grave robber limb from limb. However, if that is correct, they failed to keep out Dr Samuel Clossey, who was the head of medicine in Trinity from 1786 to 1803. This distinguished man was reputed to have also been a part-time grave robber, and even darker, may have murdered two of his own students to experiment with their bodies.

Although some of the body snatchers were amateurs who did a single shift and decided it was not the occupation for them, others were professionals who made a living out of digging up the dead. However, possibly the most despised were the medical students who dug up the bodies for their own studies. These young men employed various tricks to find fresh cadavers. One such device was to carry a false coffin filled with rocks to a graveyard and find a genuine funeral with genuine mourners. The students would mingle with authentic mourners, pass around bottles of whiskey, spiked with opium, and when the mourners were sufficiently drugged, they would exchange their coffin for the real thing. Now the students had a choice, they could take the entire coffin away, or remove the body. Most often they did the latter, dressed the corpse and staggered back to the anatomy laboratory, pretending the dead body was only dead drunk.

Stealing the dead was a strange way to begin a medical career, but the money was often essential to fund the studies of the students. At £2 for an adult corpse at a time that £1 a week was a good wage for a skilled man, body snatching could be lucrative. Children's bodies fetched less as they were valued by the inch.

Naturally, there is more to Ireland's graveyards than sack-'em-up men. Glasnevin, of course, has a ghost. This being Ireland, the spirit is not of a human being, but of a dog. Stories of loyal dogs are not uncommon. Ghosts of loyal dogs are very odd indeed. Although Ireland is an island, there seem to be relatively few sea stories compared to other maritime nations. One that has survived concerns a seaman named Captain John MacNeill Boyd.

Born in Londonderry in 1812, Boyd joined the Royal

Navy and rose to become captain of HMS *Ajax*. After service in the Baltic, he became captain of the blockship HMS *Ajax*. In February 1861 a savage storm lashed the east coast of Ireland. Captain Boyd and some his men went out to try and save the crew of the brig Neptune off Kingstown, now Dun Laoghaire. Boyd and five of his crew drowned in that storm that claimed twenty-nine vessels. The tragedy has been remembered as the Boyd Disaster, with a statue to Boyd erected in St Patrick's Cathedral, Dublin.

One version of the story says that Boyd's body was never recovered. Another says that his dog, a black Newfoundland, was at the scene. The dog followed the funeral procession and lay on Boyd's grave at Glasnevin, where it eventually joined Captain Boyd in the afterlife. Apparently, the Newfoundland has often been seen lying on the grave and can sometimes be seen patrolling the cemetery as Captain Boyd patrolled the seas.

Finally, I will add the story of the grave robbers who got a real fright. Back in 1705, long before the peak years of anatomists and resurrection men, a lady by the name of Margorie McCall of Church Place, Lurgan, wife of a surgeon named John McCall was buried in Shankhill Graveyard. A couple of shady people knew that she was still wearing her jewellery; indeed, some of the mourners mentioned one particular ring that was prominent on her finger during the wake. However, not long after she was interred, the shady ones they dug up her coffin, broke it open and tried to slide off her rings. When they failed to do so, they took out knives and began to hack her fingers from her hands. The intense pain awoke Mrs McCall from her coma, and she jerked up, screaming.

As the grave robbers fled in panic, for in that superstitious age they probably thought they had awakened some undead spirit, Margorie clambered out of her coffin, checked her ring, wondered how she got into a grave and made her unsteady way home. In another version of the story, there was only a single grave robber, and he died on the spot, and serves him right, the thieving scoundrel.

When Margorie reached her house, she found that the door was locked and knocked for entry. She heard the murmur of conversation inside and knocked again. Her husband's voice sounded clearly: 'If your mother were still alive, I'd think that was her knock.'

Rising from his place by the fire, John opened the door, to see his wife standing there in her burial gown with one finger bloody. Margorie was too slow to catch him as he fainted. Another version of the tale claims that John died of shock and was buried in Margorie's grave.

Margorie lived for many more years, and when she eventually died, she was again buried in Shankhill Graveyard, with her gravestone reading: 'Lived Once, Buried Twice.'

How was that for a strange story? Well, here is another twist. It never happened. Apparently, it is the Irish version of an old folk tale that has parallels in many other countries in Europe. The gravestone, however, is real and seems to have been erected in the nineteenth century, possibly to commemorate the story.

So that is a brief look at Irish grave robbing and some other antics that occurred in graveyards. Grave robbing was equally common in Britain at the time, but as usual, Ireland gave her own strange slant, with gun battles and still-living corpses. The next chapter will continue with the theme of the undead.

FOUR
ABHARTACH THE VAMPIRE

Most people in the western world will have heard of vampires, with Bram Stoker's Transylvanian creature Dracula as the best known. However, as Stoker was Irish, born in Clontarf, it is quite possible that he knew of an Irish vampire before he created his legendary figure. One Irish vampire was King Abhartach, who lived in what is now County Derry, east of the River Foyle in Glenullin.

Nobody is sure when Abhartach lived except that it was many centuries ago, and his title may be a courtesy one for the ruler of a small piece of land. Abhartach was not a popular man, not even among his own people, who suspected him of dabbling in the black arts. He was cruel, nasty and thoroughly unpleasant and small of stature as the name could translate as the Dwarf. However, he managed to find a wife, somehow, although he was always suspicious that she was on the lookout for a better man. Indeed, he became so confident that the poor woman was having an affair that he began to spy on her, day and night

One night he went a little too far, slid out of his window

and manoeuvred along the outside of his castle wall, hoping to catch her with another man. The wind rose, causing Abhartach to lose his footing, and he fell to the ground below. He was not discovered until morning, which suggests that his wife was indeed otherwise occupied, and by then Abhartach was dead. His people buried him quickly, in an upright position for although he had been unpopular, he was still a king, of sorts, and his rank demanded respect. That should have been the end of the unpleasant Abhartach, but instead, it was only the beginning.

Hardly had the body been buried than Abhartach was back from the dead, appearing before his erstwhile followers with a demand they cut their wrists and fill a bowl with blood for him. Too scared to argue, most complied and watched their dead king guzzle the blood as if it was the choicest ale. No sooner than Abhartach had disappeared again, the bravest of his followers ran to the neighbouring king, a man named Cathan, and asked for help.

In Ireland, the term vampire was not used. Instead, the people told Cathan that their dead king had turned into a *neamh-marbh*, which was the Irish equivalent. Cathan nodded, no doubt thinking that such a creature might well stray into his territory so had to be removed. Shortly after, Cathan hunted down Abhartach and killed him, then buried him in the correct upright position. No doubt thinking he had done an excellent job, Cathan returned home. And next day Abhartach was back with his begging bowl, demanding fresh blood. In this strange game of kill-and-recover, Cathan took his sword for another walk, despatched Abhartach again and stuck him underground for the third time. And for the third time, Abhartach came back from the dead, hungry for blood.

By now aware that killing a *neamh-marbh* was a bit pointless, Cathan looked for advice. The local lads were no good as they had no more idea than he did, so Cathan sought out a saint. As always in the old days, Ireland had more than her share of such holy men, and St Eoghan proved willing to help. Some versions of the story say that Cathan found a druid rather than a saint, and they may well be correct for that would put the story further back in time.

'Let me pray for guidance,' the saint-or-druid said.

When he had finished his praying, Eoghan advised Cathan not to kill Abhartach any more as three times was sufficient for anybody. Instead, Eoghan said, Cathan must thrust a sword made from a yew tree stake through Abhartach's heart and bury him upside down so he would not return to this realm. To make doubly sure, Cathan must cover the grave with ash branches – ash was a sacred wood – and thorns from a hawthorn bush. Finally, he had to put a large stone on top of the grave as a full stop, to keep Abhartach underground.

Cathan followed these instructions and this time Abhartach did not return. There are other versions that state Abhartach had spawned more of his kind and Cathan dedicated his life to hunting them down. Those he killed he placed inside a rath, a fairy fort, where their graves may sometimes be found. The S*idh*, the fairy folk who guard the raths, keep these vampires under control, but if the power of the Sidh should ever weaken, they will return to haunt the fair land of Ireland. That seems as good a reason to believe in fairies as any.

Abhartach's stone can still be seen. It is also a place with a strange atmosphere where strange things can happen. Perhaps it is not the best place to spend a winter night.

From the unpleasant undead, we will move on to a man who was equally abhorrent in life and much less of a myth.

FIVE

THE BLACK DOG IS LORD NORBURY

In his time, Lord Norbury was one of the most notorious men in Ireland. He was a hanging judge, the Irish Judge Jeffreys, a coarse, savage creature who joked as he sentenced men to death, ignored the suffering of others and advocated the use of torture to get confessions. All in all, he was not the sort of man you would invite home to meet your granny.

Tipperary born from an English family, Lord Norbury's given name was John Toler, and he was known for his corruption, partiality and, according to the *Dictionary of National Biography,* 'callousness and buffoonery.' So he was perhaps not the best choice to be appointed to the position of Chief Justice for the Irish Common Pleas in 1800, a position he held until 1827. Possibly his belief in the Protestant Ascendancy helped him maintain his position. Lord Norbury was also known for his wit or his gallows humour, as it may better be described. When some hopeful man asked if he could hand over a shilling to help bury a poor attorney, His Lordship flicked across a guinea, (twenty-one shillings) saying, 'Only a shilling to bury an attorney? Here's a guinea. Go and bury one-and-twenty of them.'

Another of his notorious sayings came in 1803 when the men of that year's Rising appeared before the court. Norbury tried and condemned them at great speed, so when somebody said the trials were going swimmingly, he said 'Yes, seven knots an hour.' Presumably, he was referring to the hangman's knot, a sick joke in anybody's vocabulary.

As Sir Jonah Barrington said of Lord Norbury, he 'had a hand for everybody and a heart for nobody.'

Another story that reflects the judge's callous nature says that when Norbury was returning to his mansion at Cabra from judging in the country, one of his footmen became sick. Refusing to help the man, Norbury ordered the carriage to continue to Dublin. The footman grew worse and died on the journey, so Norbury pushed him out of the carriage and left the body on the road as he drove home, or so the story goes.

Lord Norbury was particularly notorious for two cases. In one, a young man from Blanchardstown, then a small village, now a suburb of Dublin was accused of stealing sheep. Innocent or guilty, Norwood sentenced the man to death, and the execution took place. The condemned man was recently married, and his wife sickened immediately after his death. When it became evident that the wife would also die, she cursed Norbury, saying that she would haunt him for eternity, and he would never have a full night's sleep. Strangely, that is what happened as Norbury ever afterwards had terrible insomnia.

The second of Norbury's notorious cases concerns arguably the most famous personalities of Norbury's reign, Robert Emmet, who was involved in the 1803 Rising. Norbury sentenced him to be hanged, drawn and quartered. However, the Irish fates had their revenge on Norbury, for when His Lordship died, he became a *shuck*, a large black dog, cursed to roam the streets of Dublin for eternity, hauling a huge chain wherever he went. In that guise, people have frequently seen Lord Norbury, albeit not recently. He also used to be seen in his human form in his mansion at Cabra until it was demolished in the 1930s. He was not alone there, for there were other ghosts including a tall, slender and very transparent lady who could walk through closed doors. That begs the question, what happens to spirits when their old haunts are taken down? Do they haunt whatever is erected on the site? Or are they homeless as well as bodyless?

One significant kind of building where people see ghosts is a castle. Ireland has many thousands of castles and castle remains, which is a testimony to her bloody past. Some of these have had fascinating stories and a legacy of strangeness that is hard to ignore. This next chapter will look at some of Ireland's castles from a strange point of view.

SIX
SPOOKY CASTLES

WITH THOUSANDS of castles throughout Ireland, this chapter can only look at a few. The castles chosen may not be the oldest or the most famous, but, in my opinion, they all qualify for the book because of some aspect that makes them different. They are in no order of creepiness or hauntedness; I just happened to like them.

Tully Castle, County Fermanagh

Sitting on the banks of Lower Lough Erne, near Enniskillen, the ruins of Tully Castle are gaunt but still impressive. It was a Plantation castle, built in the early seventeenth century when Scottish and English Protestants settled in the north of Ireland in defiance of anything the local people thought or did. Although Tully Castle looks like a place that could defend itself against anything except a full-scale army, it fell in 1641, when the Irish rose against the unwelcome settlers in their land. The Maguire clan attacked Tully, but the castle refused to surrender. Eventually, on Christmas Eve, the captain of the castle surrendered, perhaps trusting to the sanctity of the season to protect at least the women and children who suffered inside. It was a false hope for the following day, Christmas itself, the castle was burned, with everything flammable destroyed and men, women and children dying in the flames. However, they did not leave for their spirits are still seen and heard around Christmas, lamenting their fate.

Clonony Castle, County Offaly

This fifty-foot high castle stands near Shannonbridge in County Offaly, not far from the Shannon River. Built around 1490 by the MacCoughlans, Henry VIII of England grabbed it and handed it to Thomas Boleyn, along with the title Earl of Ormond, possibly as a bribe when he wished to marry Boleyn's daughter. Of course, with her father raised to an earl, Ann Boleyn was also of a higher rank and thus suitable marriage material for royalty. Two more Boleyns, Elizabeth and Mary, lived here, giving Clonony a royal connection and keeping well out of the way of maniacal Henry with his penchant for beheading anybody to whom he took a dislike. They were lonely in Clonony, far from their English friends and unwilling to befriend the Irish. The legend states that when Elizabeth died, Mary leapt off Clonony's tower, committing suicide rather than live without her sister.

Apart from the royal connection, the castle is impressive because of the ghost of a thin man, possibly a soldier. A pale green light seems to surround him as he walks along the battlements with passing motorists able to see his light.

The castle also has a strange twirling mist and, more strangely, there are dark rumours of a cavern underneath the castle, inhabited by something dark and evil. Perhaps that is why the Boleyn sisters were buried beside a hawthorn tree, for such trees were said to be sacred to the fairy folk.

Clifden Castle, County Galway

Ireland has seen many tragic episodes in its long history, but none worse than the famine of the 1840s. Figures vary, but between one million and one and a half million people died of hunger or related diseases, and a further million emigrated. It was a tragedy that affected the national consciousness of the nation, creating bitterness that still exists, with many people blaming the British government for inaction.

One place that was directly involved is Clifden Castle. This place was built as recently as 1818. In 1845 the D'Arcy family owned the castle, and when thousands of starving tenants flocked to the castle for food or work, the owners were unwilling or unable to cope with the numbers. Many of the tenants died on the castle grounds, leaving their spirits as a reminder of these terrible times.

Charleville Castle, County Offaly

I don't think I would like to live in an ancient castle. As well as the obligatory history of bloodshed and betrayal, there will inevitably be a ghost wandering around somewhere. Charleville Castle in County Offaly is no exception. In this case, the spirit is named Harriet, and she was the youngest daughter of the Earl of Charleville. In life, Harriet seems to have been a typical, high-spirited little thing, no different from a million other children. Surprisingly, we have the actual date of her death, for, on the 8th April 1861, Harriet lifted the hem of her skirt, sat across the bannister of the impressive, twisting staircase and slid downward. Accidents are always horrible when they involve children, and Charleville Castle's was no exception, for Harriet fell and died on the floor of her own home. Her memory remains, as does her ghost, still sliding down her bannister.

Strangely, Harriet is not alone, for some have seen her playing with a mysterious young boy.

Charles Fort, County Cork

Unlike most Irish castles, Charles Fort at Kinsale is relatively modern, as the authorities built it as recently as 1682. Named after King Charles II, it is a *Trace Italienne* fortification, which was the most modern style of the period and dominates the southern edge of Kinsale Harbour. Although the current building only dates back a few centuries, it was erected on a much older site, then known as Ringcurran Castle and was primarily intended to defend Kinsale from attack by sea, so the landward defences are relatively weak, which could be why it fell after a siege of less than a fortnight in 1690. The British Army retained it as a barracks until Irish independence in 1921, and today it is popular with tourists and summer visitors.

Drifting around this seventeenth-century fort is the White Lady, who has a story of tragedy behind her. Not long after the fort was built, a Colonel Warrender was in charge. Given the position of the fort and the disturbed nature of his world, Warrender had to run a tight ship, so discipline was strict, perhaps even fierce. Even so, the colonel had the time and inclination to father a daughter, whom some versions of the story name as Wilful, a name which suggests a story in itself.

Wilful was as red-blooded as any young woman, and fell in love with an officer of the garrison, a man often named as Sir Trevor Ashurst. Strangely, Colonel Warrender allowed the match and the wedding took place without incident. On their wedding night, the happy couple took an evening stroll along the battlements to enjoy the fabulous views before repairing to bed to sleep, no doubt, until Wilful saw a single white rose growing in a crack in the wall of the fort.

Being wilful by nature as well as by name, the bride stated that she would like that rose for herself, and could Trevor please arrange things. Trevor, being a dutiful husband, agreed, but seemingly did not fancy climbing down the wall. Wilful must have been popular with the garrison, for one of the sentinels promptly volunteered to fetch the rose. As Sir Trevor took the sentries place on the battlements, the soldier tossed a rope over the wall and clambered down to pluck the rose.

In the meantime, Sir Trevor donned the sentry's uniform, took hold of the musket, sat on the battlements and promptly fell asleep, which seems a bizarre thing to do on his wedding night. He chose a bad time, for Colonel Warrender marched along the wall, checking on the vigilance of the guards. Seeing a sleeping sentry, he issued a challenge, and when the sleeping Sir Trevor did not reply, Warrender drew his pistol and shot him dead. That may sound harsh, but death was the standard penalty for a man asleep at his post at that time. Only when he looked at the body did the colonel realise he had killed his son-in-law.

In the meantime, Wilful heard the shot and came running along the battlements to see what had happened. When Wilful saw her husband lying dead on the ground, grief overcame her, and she jumped over the battlements to her death. Knowing that he had been responsible for the death of his daughter and son-in-law, Colonel Warrender shot himself that same night, or perhaps also jumped from the battlements.

Another version says that it was an ordinary soldier who married a girl in Charles Fort and he was on duty that night. He had celebrated his wedding a little too freely and fell asleep on duty, at which point an officer shot him, and his bride leapt to her death.

Either way, the result was the same. Poor Wilful remains in the fort as a spectral White Lady who wanders along the battlements. When the British army still garrisoned the fort, soldiers and their children often saw Wilful on the battlements. There are several anecdotes about her, including the story when a pair of sergeants, long-service, hard-eyed men, were working in the fort as their children played around them. The daughter of one of the sergeants asked who the white lady might be.

'What lady is that?' The sergeant asked.

'The white lady over there, the lady who is smiling at us,' the girl replied.

Both sergeants searched for the mysterious lady but saw nothing, although the children were adamant that a lady in a white dress was smiling at her. The lady is supposed to be wearing white because she was still in her wedding dress when she died, although the tradition of white weddings did not begin until the nineteenth century.

There have been other sightings, such as the nanny who saw the White Lady standing beside a sleeping child. Although the White Lady seems to like children, she is less keen on officers. Sometime in the early nineteenth century an officer, usually named as Major Black, saw her walking the ramparts in tears and much later, in 1880, two officers named as Lieutenant Hartland and Captain Marvell Hull met her as they inspected the barracks. At first, they did not know who she was until Wilful turned toward them, and they saw there was no colour in her beautiful face. More tellingly, she drifted through a closed and locked door. That same day, some unknown force, possibly Wilful, threw the officers down a flight of stairs. People have also seen Wilful in the streets of Kinsale, the town in which she may have lived.

Malahide Castle, County Dublin

Malahide Castle dates back to 1185, when the Norman-English were pushing into Ireland on their infamous land grab. King Henry II had the castle built and handed it to Sir Richard Talbot.

A jester, known as the Puck of Malahide, haunts Malahide castle, with a sad little tale attached. According to the story, the jester fancied one of the castle's prisoners, the beautiful Lady Elenora Fitzgerald. He must have told too many people, for somebody stabbed him as he left the castle, and he promised to haunt the castle thereafter. He has been frequently seen since, doing just as he promised.

In an Irish castle this old, there are naturally going to be other ghosts. One of the most commonly seen spectres is Sir Walter Galtrim, otherwise known as Sir Walter Hussey. The Husseys were one of the original Norman-English invaders of Ireland, and by the fourteenth century were well established, with branches in Meath and Kerry. Although legend has it that Sir Walter died in a battle on his wedding day sometime in the fourteenth century, I failed to find this incident. However, I did find mention of a Thomas Hussey who was reputedly murdered on his wedding day. Perhaps history and folklore have mixed the two. Either way, the ghost can still be seen in Malahide Castle.

There is more than one version of this unfortunate

ghost's death, but all seem intertwined with the attractive, Maud Plunkett, daughter of the Baron of Killeen. As in the best romances, Maud and Walter Hussey loved each other deeply, but Walter's military duties kept them apart. He also had a rival who wished to marry Maud. On the day of their wedding, Walter's rival ambushed and murdered him on his way to the church, one version claims, while the other says that the wedding took place on Whit Monday, 1429, which is in the fifteenth rather than the fourteenth century, but let's not allow facts to spoil a good story, as politicians seem to think. On the wedding day, Walter's rival murdered him. Either way, the poor lad died and, worse to come, Maud married his opponent, which is why he wanders the corridors of the castle, groaning in emotional agony.

I never did find out what happened to Maud's second-choice husband. Presumably, he died, hopefully of some horrible disease, the murdering rascal. Maud married again, this time to the Lord Chief Justice, a man whom she apparently treated very badly. According to some accounts, the poor man was the victim of some very nasty domestic abuse, with Maud assaulting him, so he had to run away with his beautiful but possibly deranged wife. Her spirit can still be met, chasing the terrified man.

There is also the ghost of a certain Miles Corbett, who seems to be as unpleasant as Maud. He was one of the men who signed King Charles I's death warrant, which may be the reason that Oliver Cromwell, an ogre in Ireland, handed Malahide Castle to him. Corbett immediately began an assault on the Roman Catholic faith, which went down well in Ireland, as one can imagine. He left Ireland at the Restoration as Charles II sought revenge for his father's execution, only to get captured, returned to Malahide and executed. In common with others at that castle, Corbett remained as a ghost, to be seen either hurrying through the castle or in a suit of armour that is said to fall into four pieces. Did people wear suits of armour in the seventeenth century?

Finally, there is my favourite Malahide ghost, the White Lady. What makes her interesting is that people can see her any time they wish, although nobody knows who she is. Her painting hangs in the Great Hall, and apparently, when she feels like a walk, the White Lady slips away from her picture to stroll the corridors and rooms of the castle. I rather like that idea.

Belvelly Castle County Cork

Lady Margaret Hodnett liked two things in the world. She loved herself, and she liked looking at herself in the mirror. That was why Belvelly Castle had a collection of the latter. Oh, and she liked men as well, and to judge by the number of hopeful suitors who flocked to Belvelly Castle, men were equally keen on Her Ladyship.

However, Her Ladyship either had a hard job making up her mind which one of her many admirers she preferred, or she simply enjoyed teasing them, for she rejected them all, time after time. Frustrated and very much attracted to the beautiful Lady Margaret, one of her admirers, Clon de Courcy, (or Lord Rockenby, take your pick of names) decided that he should take drastic measures. Whistling up his followers, de Courcy laid siege to Belvelly, ensuring that neither reinforcements nor supplies got through to the castle.

In sieges like that, time was on the side of the besiegers, and de Courcy sat tight outside Belvelly as the inhabitants of the castle grew weaker and weaker through hunger. After a year, it was evident that the castle could take no more. Many of the garrison were dead, others walking skeletons and Her

Ladyship was little better. Hunger and hardship had wasted her beauty away, so when she finally agreed to accept de Courcy's hand, he took one look at her, refused and withdrew his army.

The rejection on top of the loss of her looks broke Lady Hodnett's mind. She walked around the castle, smashing all the mirrors that once she showed her looks and died soon afterwards. Her ghost remains in the castle rubbing at the wall until it was as smooth as any mirror. However, do not expect to admire her beauty, for Her Ladyship no longer has a face, or has a veil disguising her features.

Another version of the tale claims that Lady Margaret Hodnett was captured and brought as a prisoner to the castle, where her captor starved her until her once-beautiful face was haggard and ugly. On seeing her image, Lady Margaret smashed all the mirrors in the castle. Her ghost, known as the Faceless Lady, remains.

Long before that particular Belvelly castle was built, there was a ghost at the previous building on the site. I have only found one reference to this specific ghost, so am a little wary of its existence. According to the story, there was a ship-wreck on the coast of County Cork, and the storm threw ashore a continental minstrel named Lucero Moreno. He was a handsome fellow with an eye for the ladies and a beautiful singing voice, which made him very unpopular with the then-current favourite bard, known as Dion the Thrush.

In Celtic society, the chiefs and kings were at the apex but supported poets, bards, who were maintained to praise their lords and recount their long genealogies. Bards were not merely decent singers dragged from some local pub but were trained in bardic schools, or sometimes had been the apprentice of another learned singer. Their poetry followed strict conventions of style, with compressed meaning interwoven with elegant praise that does not always correctly translate into English. It was an expression of Celtic culture that vanished after the Elizabethan and Cromwellian invasions.

Dion was especially renowned for his vocal praise of his patrons, and he also liked female company. After his long apprenticeship, Dion would be a little put out when a golden-tongued foreigner arrived to usurp his position. He would be more than annoyed when Lady Hodnett of Belvelly, one of his patrons, also fancied the younger and more handsome Moreno. The shipwrecked minstrel made the most of his time at Belvelly, seducing a whole string of women with his honeyed voice. As well as Dion, now Her Ladyship was a little upset at Moreno, notably when she witnessed his women flocking to her castle. Dion and Moreno fell out in words and deeds, much to the disharmony of Belvelly Castle.

Lady Hodnett suggested that the two men have a competition to see who the better musician was, with three songs a night for three nights. It was all much civilised and probably strange for the time, with the winner becoming the resident bard at Belvelly. When Moreno won, Dion was less than happy and attacked Moreno with his knife. However, Moreno was younger and more agile. Although wounded, he managed to kill Dion, only for Lord Hodnett to throw him into the castle's dungeon. Lying there, wounded and unhappy, Moreno gratefully accepted some food a servant girl brought to him. He was unfortunate for the girl had loved Dion, and had poisoned the food. Moreno died that same night.

According to the story, Moreno still haunts the castle. He can be seen, a handsome man singing love songs that beguile the listener so much that some cannot stand their own feelings and throw themselves in the river, or run away, never to return.

Ballygally Castle, County Antrim

Ireland seems to have a great many haunted hotels, yet Bally-gally Castle, a pleasant forty-minute drive from Belfast on the Antrim coast, stands out as a home for ghosts aplenty. There are said to be three ghosts drifting about the rooms and corridors of this beautiful place.

Any visitor may be excused for thinking they have slipped across the North Channel to Scotland, for the hotel is based around a castle built in 1625 by a Scotsman named James Shaw, who was a tenant of the Earl of Antrim. The baronial style and the inscription above the turret door, 'Godis Prividens is my Inheritans' are as Scottish as the unicorn, and to the local Irish, entirely unwelcome. When the Irish rose in 1641, they attacked the castle, without success. The original castle keep is now the centre of a luxury hotel, with a famous walled garden.

Of the ghosts, Lady Isobel or Isabella Shaw is the most often seen, or heard, for she is a mischievous spirit who likes nothing better than knocking on doors and vanishing. Her history is not so humorous, for according to legend, her husband kept her prisoner in a small room in the tower and starved her. She fell or perhaps jumped out of a window to her death. As Lady Isobel is searching for her daughter, maybe she is not playing when she knocks on doors. Her presence lowers the temperature, and those who sense her are often aware of strange smells. The turret room in which her husband confined her is now known as the Ghost Room. Perhaps fortunately, the hotel does not use it for guests.

One hotel manager spoke about a guest in a room beneath the Ghost Room, who heard children laughing in his room and fled wearing only his underwear. The manager also mentioned setting up a table in the Dungeon Room, only to return later and find the napkins unfolded and the glasses set in a circle, as if ready for a séance.

Madame Nixon is a second ghost. She lived in the castle in the nineteenth century and is heard walking around with her silk dress rustling.

Strangely, sometimes the Otherworld sends the hotel a warning that something is going to happen, in the shape of a green mist that appears outside the castle. Be wary of the mist!

Killua Castle, County Westmeath

Killua Castle looks like it would be the perfect place for a gothic horror story. It stands at Clonmellon, County Westmeath, a large house with a twisted history. It was owned by the Chapman family, originally from Leicestershire, with Thomas Chapman, 2nd Baron Killua making considerable alterations to the castle.

So far, nothing strange then, except maybe the 1810 obelisk near the house that shows where the English mariner and relative of the Chapmans, Walter Raleigh, planted potatoes from the New World, starting Ireland's love-hate relationship with that crop. More strange is the ghost that can sometimes be seen drifting around. According to legend, it is the spirit of Jacky Dalton, an eighteenth-century land steward who stole a large sum of money from the Chapmans. He was a smart crook, but not so bright that he profited by his thefts, for he drank away what he gained before drowning himself.

A small man, Dalton seems to be an unfriendly kind of ghost that scares people away from the house, although he may not be the ugly looking apparition or the figure in white.

Not quite strange but undoubtedly worth a mention is

the castle's connection to one of the most enigmatic figures of the First World War. The last Chapman to live in Killua was Thomas, who moved across the Irish Sea and changed his surname name to Lawrence. His son was T. E. Lawrence, who is better known as Lawrence of Arabia, that enigmatic figure who helped raise the Arabs to fight the Ottoman Empire during the 1914 – 1918 War.

SEVEN
GOLFING WITH THE FAIRIES

Coming from Scotland, I thought I knew all about golf. After all, the Scots invented the game and have the oldest and some of the most scenic courses in the world. I believe Scotland has more golf courses per head of population than anywhere else, so it is hard to find any Scottish town without at least one course. In saying that, Ireland is nearly as prolific with her courses and I had never before come across a golf course that included a fairy tree. That was one up for the island of Ireland.

Ormeau Golf Club is in the heart of Belfast, a nine-hole course that can challenge even serious golfers, let alone hackers such as me. The club was formed in 1893 and is one of the oldest in Belfast, and with a view of cranes of the shipyard where *Titanic* was built, one of the most unique. The course itself is a delight, parkland with individual trees on land that was owned by the Marquis of Donegall as part of his Ormeau demesne.

On the third hole, cunningly named Fairy Thorn, there sits a thorn tree, which my fellow golfers advised me to miss.

(One man, tired of playing with a blundering amateur, said the opposite, 'hit the damned thing,' he said. 'You can't get any worse than you are.') Apparently, the little people, the fairies, the *Sidh*, still live on or in this tree and strongly object when a golfer cracks his ball against their home. If the errant golfer is lucky, the fairies will accept an apology. If he or she is unlucky, then the penalty could be dire indeed. After a life-time of living with strange things and searching for unusual events, I was not surprised when one of my golfing compan-ions took off his cap and nodded to the tree. I did the same of course, partly so that I did not appear churlish, but also because one never knows, especially in Ireland.

'It's a bit ragged for a fairy tree,' I resented that crack about my lack of golfing skill. 'Should you not give it a bit of a trim?'

'No,' my companion shot me down in flames. 'The green-keepers leave it sincerely alone.' He gave me a look that the Gorgon would envy. 'If you insult it even, you'll lose the game, and if your ball ends up in the tree, you leave it.'

My ball neither hit the tree nor landed in the branches, but I still gave the hawthorn my respects. It did me no good, of course, I lost the game very badly, which is not unusual for me.

At a hundred-and-twenty years old, the thorn has not yet reached middle age, for hawthorns can last for four hundred years and reach about twenty feet tall, not tall as trees grow, but surely a significant hazard for any golf course. While some people thought that fairies lived in these trees, others said the little people only gathered there. I have insufficient evidence to dispute either point of view.

That was my first encounter with a fairy thorn tree, but as I sat in the Fairy Tree Bistro afterwards, listening to the *craic* and ignoring the banter about my atrocious round, I happened to mention the fairy thorn. I expected the subject to be laughed off or ignored, but on the contrary, the people took the issue seriously, if in a light-hearted manner. If that sounds strange, then remember that this was Ireland, where the gift of the blarney is expected, and women and men can jest about anything in all seriousness.

My golfing companions told me that the island of Ireland has many such fairy thorn trees which are best to avoid. Now, I am quite fond of wandering around the countryside over hills and through fields, so I asked how I could recognise these dangerous trees. The answer was simple: The fairy thorns are commonly isolated thorn trees that grow all alone, at the side of the road or in the middle of a field. They remain there, untouched, even if the farmer has to plough or sow around them when it would be far easier to uproot the tree and have an open field with unrestricted access for a tractor. For generations, possibly for centuries, people have believed that if anybody cuts these trees down, or damages them in any fashion, bad luck will result, even to an early death. The Irish fairies are not to be taken lightly. As I have declared above, they are the *Sidh*, from the old people who were here before the Celts, renowned for their magic and grace.

The belief in fairy trees stretches back to pre-Christian times, for the hawthorn was sacred to the Celts. The Irish, different in most things, also called the hawthorn the lone bush, lone thorn or even the gentle bush, for it was best not to say the name 'fairy' for fear of causing offence, so a form of early political correctness. At the ancient Celtic Beltane festival at the beginning of summer, on the other hand, the hawthorn trees were often decorated, so presumably, the little people joined in the festivities. To Christians, the hawthorn is said to be the tree that supplied the crown of thorns that the Romans fixed on Christ's head during the crucifixion.

This religious usage would make the hawthorn doubly sacred unless the early Christians merely hijacked the old Celtic beliefs.

I was told that there are prominent and famous fairy trees at St Brigid's Well in County Kildare, on the famous Hill of Tara in Meath, in Connemara's Killary Harbour and Ben Bulbin in Sligo.

Despite the antiquity of the fairy beliefs, there have been some high-profile incidents concerning the trees in recent years, as I found out from various people. Perhaps the strangest case was in 1999 when a major road was being built from Galway to Limerick. Construction halted when the engineers found that a fairy tree stood square in the chosen route. Rather than uproot the tree, the planners chose a new route, the road was a decade late, and the tree left severely alone. I have never heard of such a thing happening in any other country, but in Ireland, tradition runs deep and no harm in that at all.

Ten years later, in 2009, there was another incident concerning a fairy tree, this time on the Mullaghmoyle Road near Coalisland in County Tyrone. When a well-known fairy tree beside the crumbling ruins of an ancient farmhouse was cut down, there were repercussions in the form of a ghost. She was said to be a lady dressed all in white, and people came to Coalisland to see this unusual phenomenon. As always in such cases, there were various versions of the story, with some locals claiming the ghost had only appeared since the hawthorn was removed and others saying it had been around for centuries. However, the spirit made international news, with papers from London also showing interest. Purely for research purposes and for no other reason, I popped into the hostelry at Coalisland to ask the local punters what they thought. Unfortunately, I must have chosen the wrong time to come, or news of my lack of golfing prowess had spread, for the only man who proved willing to talk said he had never seen any ghost and cared nothing if they chopped down every hawthorn tree in Ireland. He suggested I return ten years ago. It was a different situation back in 2009, apparently, or at least according to the newspaper reports.

If my personal searching proved less than useful, the people at Coalisland Library proved more than helpful. They pointed me in the right direction, so I learned another use, or perhaps reason, for fairy trees and one that was vaguely disturbing. Apparently, there is a belief that some of the fairy trees were deliberately planted, rather than being placed by nature. A priest, Roman Catholic or possibly Druid, would exorcise an evil spirit from somebody, trap it in a bottle and bury it underground, planting a thorn tree on top as a marker to warn people off. The fairy stories evolved as a better way to keep the tree from being disturbed, which might release the evil spirit. The nearest thing I had heard was the *djinns* of the East who were trapped in lanterns, and I wondered if there was a single source for such beliefs. With our major religions originating from the Middle East, many superstitions could also have come from there. . But that is to leave Coalisland before I have quite finished with that fairy-tree ghost...

While some of the locals claimed to have seen the woman in white on a nearly daily basis, others were fairly offhand, saying 'it's nothing great, only a ghost.' I was vaguely surprised that even a ghost could become part of normality in Ireland. Only a very strange place could be so accepting of the supernatural.

The Coalisland Fairy Tree is, or was, only one of many such trees across Ireland. As well as hawthorn, fairy trees can be ash or even mountain ash, otherwise known as rowan.

Rather than stand in splendid isolation in fields, some fairy trees can hug the roadside, or are in some significant ancient site or even beside a holy well, which makes sense.

Naturally, there are two sides to every folklore coin, so if it is unlucky to cut down a fairy tree, it is also conversely lucky to have one on one's land. Some farmers ensured their fairy trees were safe by piling boulders around the trunks to keep away unpleasant people with saws, axes and such-like implements of tree-destruction, although there are stories that it was the fairies who moved these boulders to protect their homes.

At one time, and possibly even today, people visit the fairy trees to leave small gifts or offer prayers to the fairies, hoping for better health, wealth or fortune. Presumably, this form of tree worship was higher at the time of Beltane when the tree was in full bloom. The little people were looked on with a mixture of fear and awe, mainly because they were believed to have supernatural powers, and that brings us to another belief about the fairy trees. As the fairies were denizens of a world that was not quite solid yet not supernatural, it was assumed that fairy trees acted as a doorway between the two. It was possible to use the trees to enter the fairy world, or, as sometimes the trees were beside ancient burial mounds, the mounds were the gateway to this Otherworld. Naturally, there are nearly as many theories about the fairies as there are fairy trees, but one concerns another strange and possibly mythical race of people in Ireland. Apparently, sometime in the past, a people known as the Milesians invaded Ireland from Spain. At that time the indigenous peoples of the island were the *Tuatha de Danaan*, the Children of Danu. The Milesians- presumably the Celts- defeated the Tuatha de Danaan, who withdrew underground. These old people were small in stature and possessed supernatural powers. They became known as the *Sidh*, the fairies, who travelled between their new world underground and this upper world through ancient burial mounds or through the fairy trees. There may be a great deal of truth in these old legends, for some anthropologists believed that the Neolithic people and the Bronze-age people who joined them were smaller in stature than that Celts who displaced them. One theory suggests that these ancient peoples lived in small communities in houses sunk into the ground, roofed with turf. They used bronze tools and flint-headed arrows and were excellent poets, musicians and magicians. Defenceless against the iron weapons of the Celts, they fought back by moving at night, using their magic and stealing their children.

There is also a possibility that there was nothing mythological about the trees at all, but the old folk knew how useful the berries and flowers are for medicinal purposes and did not wish the trees destroyed for that reason. These wise women and men invented the Sidh stories to help protect these most useful trees. In Ireland, the truth hides behind a tapestry of mythology and legend that adds colour to every square inch of the island. Even today people make a wish when they pass a fairy thorn, and to give a relatively recent and well-known example, when the DeLorean factory was built at Dunmurry near Belfast, the builders are said to have chopped down a fairy thorn. Apparently, one of the managers actually listened to the workers' worries and replaced the tree with another, but it evidently was not to the fairies liking. The *Sidh* had their revenge and DeLorean is no more in Dunmurry.

Is it possible that an ancient fairy curse destroyed that fantastic futuristic vehicle? In Ireland, it may well be. There are other similar instances, such as one in Downpatrick, possibly in the early years of the twentieth century. Builders were ordered to erect a house in a field where a fairy thorn stood. When the workers refused to knock down the tree, the foreman realised he had no choice but to act alone. After he started to haul at the roots, he became aware of a white mouse at his feet, and then another, and more and more of them. Even the iron will of the foreman quailed at the sight, for surely these mice were the manifestations of the fairies themselves.

Nevertheless, he continued to work on, dragging the tree trunk aside and loading the soil into a wheel-barrow. As he wheeled the barrow away, a horse panicked for some reason, knocking him down, so he broke a leg. In fact, the leg was so severely damaged that it had to be amputated. Dark tales circulated that the fairies scared the horse. That theory would fit in with old folk stories that claimed that men who tried to chop down hawthorns found their axe would refuse to cut the wood, sometimes turning in the user's hand to decapitate him.

I was told that witches were also said to make their broomsticks from the branches of a hawthorn and when I mentioned that to my good wife, she told me that she remembered smelling hawthorn blossom as a girl. She called it a very evocative smell, which ties in with the Irish theory that men find hawthorn blossom erotic. Possibly that is why Maypoles, that ultimate symbol of eroticism, were once made from hawthorn trees. There is the old theory that if you were foolish enough to fall asleep under a fairy tree, or even any old hawthorn tree, you might wake up in fairyland. That doesn't sound too bad, with feasting and dancing, while the fairy men are as handsome as the fairy women are beautiful, but be careful. Time flies in the Otherworld, and what seems like a night there could be a whole year in this realm, or a great deal longer. You might come back to find all your relatives and friends long dead and buried.

As well as the hawthorn, other trees also have Otherworldly reputations, but rather than ethereal witches, the blackthorn had an association with the winter goddess and the less savoury side of witches. Better known is the rowan, whose branches or berries protected animals, byres and even children from witches and fairies.

We are now a long way from the golf course in Belfast so I will end with a small and well-known anecdote from W. B. Yeats, the poet and politician. In the early years of the twentieth century, Yeats was wandering through Sligo when he asked an old man if he believed in fairies. After a vigorous and nearly indignant denial, the elderly man said, 'I don't believe in them at all, but they're there.'

I think that even now in the twenty-first century, many Irish people would agree with the old gentleman's statement. After hearing the stories, I might be inclined to be the same.

EIGHT
STRANGE IRISH CREATURES

AFTER THE FAIRY TREES, it seems natural to talk about other strange creatures that were once thought to inhabit the island of Ireland. There are many of them; indeed, there are so many that it is surprising that they could all fit in one comparatively small island. First of all, we will look at one of Ireland's most famous symbols.

The Leprechauns

Ireland is famous for many things, but the leprechauns are perhaps the most readily identifiable icon of Irishness. These little green-clad men appear in tourist brochures, booklets and other items that promote anything Irish. They are usually depicted as elderly men with green clothes and ornately buckled shoes, and it is the shoes that provide a hint as to their original identity. They have evolved from cobblers.

Dublin even has a Leprechaun Museum in Jervis Street, where one can be transported to a different world on the words of enchanting storytellers. When my wife and I were there, a lady named Naoise gave us a delightful tour of Irish folklore and legend. It was all meat and drink to me, of course, but it would be even better for children, but that is to stray from this little piece about Leprechauns.

As I stated already, the first leprechauns were shoemakers, cobblers. However, that is not their claim to fame. They travel about Ireland collecting gold, which they bury at the end of a rainbow. Now, as Ireland has a maritime climate, it has been known to rain from time to time, so rainbows are not an uncommon occurrence. So all one has to do is follow the rainbow, mark the end and dig. When you find the pot of gold, don't forget to thank the leprechaun who buried it there, or he might be most offended.

These little green fellows have magic powers, of course. If anybody catches one, the leprechaun has to grant three wishes. Not all leprechauns will be willing to oblige, however, so be prepared for tricks.

In Killough, north Westmeath, a leprechaun appeared in the spring of 1908. Small of stature, dressed in red rather than green, and with a peaked cap, people saw him for a few moments, and then he vanished with a mocking laugh. Although newspapers in the supposedly more sophisticated areas of Ireland and Great Britain pretended amusement at the story, perhaps there was an element of wishful thinking, or even belief, behind the scepticism.

I have a couple of little anecdotes (out of hundreds) about the antics of leprechauns. As late as the 1920s, some people in Ireland still believed in leprechauns and fairies. A Mr Patterson of Belturbet, County Cavan related the following small story: 'it was one night I went to bring the cows in. In the field where they grazed there was a little patch which if they went on to it, they would never give milk afterwards.'

Mr Patterson said that he suspected that either

leprechauns or fairies had cursed that patch of grass. On that particular night: 'Suddenly I came upon a little leprechaun, or he let me come upon him. He took to his heels and ran, but dropped his little shoe as he went. I chased him, but lost him in some bushes.'

Mr Patterson returned home to tell his cousin John. One of Patterson's beliefs was that they could not kill a fairy, leprechaun or ghost unless you shot them with a silver sixpence. Patterson and John heated up a couple of silver sixpences until they were malleable, and hammered them into the rough shape of bullets. Loading his gun with the silver bullets, Patterson got himself ready to return.

'We climbed the hill to where I had seen the wee leprechaun and all of a sudden, we came upon a fairy dance in full swing.' Patterson swore that he was telling the truth. He had no reason to lie: Why fabricate a story that he knew would cause people to scoff at him?

'And there was the little leprechaun fairy that I'd seen before, standing playing the music. It wasn't a flute or anything. It was one of the reeds that grew in the field.'

Patterson did not use his gun. He mentioned another occasion when he saw the fairies or leprechauns when he lay on a haystack. 'We lay and watched them for a couple of minutes and then came back down the hill.'

So we will never know if the silver bullets would have worked or not. We only know that the belief in leprechauns lasted at least until the twentieth century.

Even later and possibly more disturbing, was the supposed revival of leprechaun belief around Carlingford as late as 1989. According to the story, a local man found a small green suit and a handful of gold coins on Foy Mountain. In 1991 a Leprechaun Whisperer named Kevin Woods said he had spoken to a leprechaun named Carraig, who was the elder leprechaun of the 236 who remained in the area. True? Well, if anybody is unsure, they are welcome to join in the annual leprechaun hunt that takes place here. Happy hunting, and remember, if people stop believing in them, leprechauns will become extinct, and nobody wishes that to happen.

Another of the supernatural creatures that haunt, or haunted, Ireland was the Banshee.

The Banshee

Banshees, in different names, seem to appear in folklore in various Celtic countries. In Ireland, the name comes from the Gaelic, *bean-sidhe*, which could mean a woman of the sacred one or woman of the fairy. I prefer the latter translation, even though there is not much to pick between them. Although there are Banshees, with different names, in Scotland and Brittany, Ireland seems to be their spiritual home, and only in Ireland was the fairy sickness once known.

If a man or woman fell, he or she would immediately jump up and turn three times sunwise, then dig out a chunk of earth or turf because the earth reflects one's shadow. If the man or woman becomes sick within the next few days, somebody has to fetch a wise woman to remove this *esane* – the fairy sickness.

In some accounts, the Banshees only appeared to five major Irish families, the O'Connors, the O'Neils, O'Bryons, Kavanaghs and O'Gradys, and was not a popular visitor as she, or it, warns of impending death. Her, or its, cry often comes at night, while the actual Banshee can appear in several guises, notably a crow or a stoat. Both animals were disliked in Celtic Ireland and in later mythology were both associated with witchcraft.

In other accounts, the Banshee appears as a woman, often with long hair, dressed in a long grey cloak over a green tunic. Green is the Celtic magic or fairy colour and occurs in many supernatural beings. The Banshee has also been described as red-haired, dressed in white and red-eyed. There seem to be as many descriptions of Banshees as there are Banshees themselves.

The Banshee could be the spirit of a woman who died young and virginal, mourning the life she could have had. One distinguished gentleman in the Mutton Lane Inn in Cork informed me that the Banshees were usually seen beside the river, washing the bloody shroud of those about to die. Nevertheless, I read that Banshees were women who flew through the air, weeping. To add to the confusion, the Banshee is either very tall or very short, but always seems to keen, or wail. That was her job, of course for it was said that if the Banshee's wail is heard three times outside a house, one person inside will die.

I tried to find out the origin of the Banshees, but nobody seems to know. Perhaps they have always been in Ireland, howling at night and warning people of impending death. Maybe they have not always been there. Perhaps they are supernatural birds, as some believe. Perhaps they are indeed the spirits of women who died in childbirth, or who died too young, as other people think.

So nobody is sure from where the Banshee legends come. Does anybody know their purpose, except to create an unearthly noise? Well, they also carry a negative atmosphere, for wherever Banshees are, there is melancholy and gloom. It is possible that they haunt funerals and warn of impending death because they are permanently mourning their own premature death.

But there is an alternative possibility. Another theory claims that the Banshees are neither the spirits if birds of humans but are from the old race of *Tuatha De Danaan*, hence their other-worldly powers and, indeed, the name.

There is said to be a Banshee at the harbour of Newcastle, County Down, drifting among the boats, possibly warning the fishermen of the dangers of the trade in which they are involved.

While I was in the Mutton Lane Inn talking to my new friend, his companion told me that Banshees were all nonsense and they never existed. This spoilsport insisted that people mistook the call of hunting vixens for the cry of the Banshee. I was not convinced. I wanted to believe in the Banshees, to have something from the Otherworld waiting out there in the dark.

The Pooka

I must confess that I had never heard of a Pooka before I visited Ireland. It seems to be a strange creature that could be a fairy or other beast of the night. Sometimes they are huge black eagles or some humanoid monster, although the most common form seems to be a black horse that runs riot in the hours of darkness, destroying everything in its path, stopping hens from laying and cows from producing milk.

What was even more unpleasant about Pookas was their ability to alter their shape. At night they could be a horse while during the day they could turn into a Goblin or other unpleasant creature. Knowing of their habits, farmers often left a corner of their fields ungathered so that the Pooka would take the free grain rather than destroy everything. On a sinister note, the Pooka could wait outside the house and call on the people inside. If any of the inhabitants left the house, the Pooka grabbed them for some unpleasant purpose, while if the people resisted the invitation, the Pooka would destroy everything that it could.

If the Pooka were in the shape of a horse, it could walk up to some unsuspecting human, lower its head and thrust it between its victim's legs, then toss him onto its back. With the victim thus trapped, the Pooka galloped away. Once, very many years ago, a merchant came to Larconnaught on business. Allowing his horse to graze in the fields behind his lodgings, he slept well, awoke early and stumbled to find his horse. Unable to see properly in the dark, he inadvertently mounted a Pooka, which trotted away with him. After a few moments, the Pooka speeded up, galloping and leaping to throw his rider and break his neck, only for the merchant to wrap his hands around the Pooka's mane and hang on all the tighter. It was then that the merchant remembered he was wearing spurs and dug them into the Pooka, harder and harder until the creature's blood flowed and begged the rider to desist.

'Not until you take me safely back,' the merchant said, spurring with even more venom than before. 'And promise not to molest any other innocent traveller.'

'I'll do that,' said the Pooka. 'I promise I'll do that.' Taking the merchant back to the field behind his lodgings, it ran away. The merchant was never bothered again, and nobody ever saw that Pooka in Larconnaught again.

The Pooka has left its mark in place names around Ireland, with one, Poulaphouca on the River Liffey in County Wicklow, now a spot for tourists. The name could mean the Pooka's Pool or The Ghost's Hole. In the late 1930s and early 1940s, the Liffey was dammed here to create a reservoir and a hydro-electric power station, but Poulaphouca survived, while the reservoir submerged other small villages. Interestingly, low water levels have allowed archaeologists to dig at these abandoned villages, and they have uncovered objects from as far back as the Mesolithic period as well as from the Neolithic, Iron and Bronze Age. Could it be that the Pooka is a warning about people from the distant past?

There is also Carrigaphooca, the Pooka's Rock or, as some would have it, the Castle on the Rock of the Fairy, near Macroom in County Cork. The Castle was founded in the sixth century, with many later additions, while the name Macroom is said to mean 'the gathering place of the followers of Crom.' This particular Celtic deity, *Crom Cruach* is a bit of a mystery, with a name that can translate as 'bowed one of the mound', or 'head of the stack of corn' or simply 'bloody head.' Human sacrifices could have been made to Crom Cruach, or he could simply have been a fertility god or a sun god. Whatever he was, St Patrick is said to have sorted him out, so the world is safer now. There are stories that Druids met at Macroom, while the Castle is said to be haunted by a man named Cormac whose fate was to be damned for eternity for becoming a cannibal. More in keeping with the subject in hand, the Castle also has a Pooka, in this case not so much a horse as a dark thing that can attack people – could that be a memory of the god Crom? Nearby is a megalithic stone circle, another reminder that Pooka sites are often near ancient monuments.

When they were not terrorising innocent travellers or haunting castles, Pookas had other tricks up their sleeves. People blamed Pookas for spoiling the blackberries every 29th

September, so that nobody could pick them after that date. But be of good cheer, travellers all, for the Pooka only exists at night time. As soon as the first cock crows in the morning, they vanish from our world.

The Merrow

Have you ever heard of a Merrow? I had not. It seems to be a bit like a mermaid, although the name is said to mean sea-maid. Unlike the mermaid, Merrows have legs like humans, although their feet are flat and their fingers are webbed.

Merrows are strange creatures, indeed. In some parts of Ireland, they seem to wear a red-feather in their cap, which enables them to travel through the sea. Other accounts say the sealskin cape that they wear give them their powers. In either case, their strength is also a weakness, for if they wish to walk like a human being, they must cast aside their hat or cape. In the few cases that I came across, Merrows were always females, which must make reproduction difficult and possibly explains why nobody has seen any recently.

Like the Scottish selkies, Merrows are beautiful creatures and men used to wish them for wives. Not only were they beautiful, but they can also be wealthy as they scour the sea bed for treasure, both natural and salvaged from sunken ships. The husband has to be careful, though, for the pull of the ocean is powerful, and if the Merrow finds her cape and hat, she will return to her watery home.

Kelpies

Kelpies appear in both Irish and Scottish folklore. If you happen to be walking near a river, you may be tempted to pet any friendly-looking horse that ambles up, slightly damp and very appealing. That might be safe. You may also be tempted to leap on its back for a free ride around the locality. Here is a piece of free advice from Uncle Jack Strange – resist the temptation! That friendly horse may well be a Kelpie, so once you are on its back, you will be stuck there, unable to dismount. In that way, they are similar to the Pookas, if even more dangerous.

The Kelpie will take you on a wild ride into the nearest river and down, into the depths. When the Kelpie has drowned you, it will turn into a voracious beast that eats you, all except for the liver and heart which, for some reason, it does not like.

Sometimes the Kelpie can appear as a human, either a handsome, dark-haired man (if its chosen victim happens to be female) or a glossy-haired woman (if its victim is a male.) Don't be deceived; beneath the disguise, Kelpies are still the nasty horse-creatures. They do have a weakness, though. If you happen to find their silver bridle, you can keep them on land, although why you would want to associate with such unpleasant creatures, I cannot imagine.

The Sidh

The generic name for Ireland's fairies, the Sidh live in fairy mounds, gather in fairy trees and sometimes in fairy rings and are to be treated with respect at all times. If you happen to come across one, walk warily and be respectful. How can you recognise them? Well, there is an elegant description of Edain the Fairy in a ninth century text, far too long to be written here. What follows is a shortened version:

'Her upper arms were as white as the snow of a single night, and they were soft and straight, and her clear and lovely cheeks were as red as the foxglove of the moor. The bright blush of the moon was in her noble face... The ray of love-making in both her royal eyes... A gentle womanly dignity in her voice. She was the fairest and loveliest and most perfect of the women of the world.'

So there you are; we have a fairy queen but as Kipling advises, 'walk wide' for her smile can ensnare you, her beauty enchant you and her wiles, trap you forever in her world.

Changelings

Changelings are heavily associated with fairies and as such are best avoided. Irish fairies, the *Sidh*, you see, are not like Tinkerbell in *Peter Pan*. They can be vindictive creatures who steal babies and leave a wrinkled and malformed fairy-child in its place. These stories may have begun the worry about changelings, so the old-time Irish mothers were cautious with new-born children, guarding them at all times and placing rowan twigs around the doorway, for fairies hate rowan.

A changeling can also be an old fairy in disguise. Again, be careful. And thirdly, not all children are children. Fairies can alter the appearance of anything to make it look like a child – even like your beloved baby. Now that explains how a perfectly normal, happy child can alter into a moody, irritable, disobedient monster – and all this time we blamed it on puberty.

If you are unfortunate enough to have a Changeling rather than your own child, you will soon know. They yell a lot, complain about everything and are happiest when things go wrong inside the family into which they have moved, again, much like pubescent teenagers. However, there is hope. Also in common with teenagers and many fairies, Changelings like music. If you are lucky, you may win their trust with music, while if you are unlucky, they will enchant you through the power of music. Whatever you do, don't allow a Changeling to entice you to follow them into a mound or a fairy circle. Once inside, you may never be able to leave.

One notorious Changeling case occurred as recently as 1895. I know that sounds like rather a long time ago, but in Ireland, with its incredibly long history, 1895 is just the other day. That year, Michael Cleary murdered his wife, later claiming that she was not his wife at all. He said that fairies had abducted the woman he married and left a Changeling in her place. Unfortunately for a bizarre story, the judge did not agree and sentenced Cleary to fifteen years for manslaughter. I wonder if Cleary genuinely believed his defence, or if he was hoping the judge was a man with old-fashioned ideas.

Leanan Sidhe

As you'll know by now, Ireland has a plethora of strange fairies and monsters. One of the most unusual is surely the *Leanan Sidhe*. This creature appears to musicians and poets as a beautiful woman and offers inspiration. Naturally susceptible to beauty and hope, men of such artistic talents soon fall under the spell of the Leanan Sidhe. They would become lovers, sharing her bed and learning from her intelligence and magic. When the Leanan Sidhe has had enough of them, she would leave. Suffering from a broken heart, the artists would slide into depression and eventually die.

That was what the Leanan Sidhe had been planning. She would drag the dead artist back to her home and there, hidden from the world, she would drain their blood. The Leanan Sidhe had a huge cauldron in which she collected the blood of all the artists, writers and musicians with whom she had made love. From that blood, she drew her skills and talents as well as her beauty, with the power of her lover's words adding to her own.

Another version of the Leanan Sidh is as a fairy lover. Fingin MacLuchta, King of South Munster in the second century AD was said to have a Leanan Sidh who visited him every Samain, (now called Halloween) and took him to her fairy palace. Another king, Fachna of Ulster, had a Sidh who foretold the future.

Now, if you are in any way artistically minded, you will wish to avoid the Leanan Sidhe, so all you have to do to keep her down is find her grave and create a cairn of stones on top. Good luck with that!

Gancanagh

The Gancanagh is another Irish fairy that it is best to avoid. It arrives in the shape of a handsome man to seduce any woman who takes its fancy. Naturally, it has supernatural powers to achieve its objective, so the chosen woman has little chance to resist. Once the woman is hopelessly smitten, the fairy lover will vanish. That does not sound so bad, except that even when he is gone, the fairy's powers over the woman will continue, binding her to it forever.

The Gancanagh has also been called the Love-singer and was reputed to enchant lone women such as milkmaids, make love to them and then vanish.

Alp-luachra

That Gaelic name translates as 'joint-eater'; this is a nasty little fairy that looks just like a newt. This little demon enters the mouth of its victim and stays there, eating any food that is stuffed in until the victim starves to death. I did not find out much about this creature and, to be honest, I don't think I wanted to.

Far Darrig

The Far Darrig was another creature I had never heard of until I wandered around Ireland. These curious creatures seem to be a cross between a leprechaun and a fairy. The name means red man, possibly because they wear a red hat and coat. They are supremely nasty creatures who inspire nightmares; perhaps they creep inside one's head and tell unpleasant stories. They also carry sacks in which to carry the people they kidnap, help fairies steal babies and project their voices into scary sounds. They are best avoided, then.

Stories about the Far Darrigs seem to come with various themes. One strange one is when the Far Darrigs entice humans into their home and ask them to cook a meal. However, when the human enters the kitchen, he or she will see an old woman impaled on a spit above the fire, which is probably not the best way to start a meal. However, if you are wise, you can avoid such ugly encounters; as soon as you suspect the creature you are with is a Far Darrig, you can say 'you cannot mock me' which stops them dead. My mentions of Far Darrigs in pubs across Ireland did not receive much of a reaction, so I suspect belief in such things has considerably waned.

Fear Gorta

I doubt anybody in the western world has not heard of zombies. They are a strangely popular type of monster just now, with a whole host of books and films available. Well, they are not a modern invention, nor, as some believe, do they come exclusively from West Africa or even the Caribbean. The Irish have had them for many centuries.

Perhaps the stories originated during one of the many famines that have hit Ireland over the centuries, for the Fear Gorta certainly sound like starving people. Writers have described them as walking corpses with their bones visible through rotting flesh and blue skin as they ask anybody for food. If you provide food, the world will reward you with prosperity; if you refuse, then poverty will surely follow. To this Strange Jack, that sounds like a reminder that charity is its own reward and a request to help those in need.

However, there is another version of the Fear Gorta legend that claims some graves have a cursed area of grass on top. If you step on that cursed section, then lifelong hunger will result. That myth is suspiciously similar to the legend that claims anyone stepping on the grave of a famine victim will be cursed. Perhaps it is a method of keeping the memory of those terrible days alive

The Dullahan

We are on more familiar territory with the Dullahan, as it is a headless horseman, another figure that seems prevalent in both Ireland and Scotland. In Ireland, the Dullahan rides a black horse and wears a black cloak, with his head held in his right hand. In his left hand, he whips the horse with a human spine, which makes one wonder how he manages to control the horse. Presumably, he has very educated knees and thighs. He is always a dark, morose person, sometimes a Goblin or some such. He may also ride a coach.

When people heard the rumble of the iron-shod wheels and the drumbeat of hooves on the ground, they looked away, huddled over their fires or hurriedly closed windows or doors for nobody wished to see the Dullahan. In Munster, the Dullahan was said to be familiar to specific families, riding the fatal coach to the front door of the house when death was imminent.

This evil creature is a death omen as it gallops around the spot where the death is to be, shouting the name of he who is about to die. All the time he rides, the Dullahan holds his head by the hair, watching for the victim. If you see one, hide, for if the Dullahan sees you looking, he will crack you in the eye with his whip or spray you with blood. Some versions claim that the horse has fiery eyes, or says that if the horseman sees you yet continues to ride, you are safe. The second that he stops, however, somebody will die.

There is one way to escape; it seems that the Dullahan is scared of gold, so if he threatens you with his fierce whip, or tries to spray you with blood, simply flip a gold coin at him. That should send him back to hell or whatever stable from which he came. Unfortunately, my stock of gold coins is always a bit thin – that comes from having a wife, you see.

Dearg Due

I doubt that anybody in the western world has not heard about Dracula, read the book or seen one of the many, many films. I have already mentioned that Bram Stoker, who created Dracula, was Irish. He undoubtedly was inspired by the legends of Transylvania, but it is also possible that the stories of the Dearg Due influenced him.

Dearg Due is a Gaelic name that means red blood sucker, which is a perfect name for a vampire. In Ireland, the Dearg Due is a female that attracts men, smiles nicely and sucks out their blood. One story seems old and strangely familiar. Very many years ago, there was an incredibly beautiful woman. Men came from all across Ireland to woo her, much to her father's satisfaction, who sought a rich husband for her. However, the woman fell in love with a poor man instead.

In those bad old days, love had little to do with marriage. Young women had no say who they married, so the father found his rich bridegroom and forced his daughter into matrimony. The husband was as cruel as he was rich and preferred the company of women of loose morals to his wife. After a few years of torment, the husband locked her in a tower. The bride remained there, hoping her true love would come to rescue her. When days passed, and nobody came, the bride decided she did not want to live in a horrible marriage, so starved herself to death.

Either her husband or her father buried the woman beside Strongbow's Tree in Waterford, which was perhaps not the quietest spot to choose as Strongbow was one of the original Norman-English invaders of Ireland. The tree is meant to have grown next to Reginald's Tower at the city quay. At any rate, the lady, or something that had taken her form, arose from the grave and drifted to her father's house. When she requested admittance, he stared at her, unbelieving, and allowed her in. As anybody with knowledge of vampires knows, inviting one in gives it power within the house and the woman, no longer human, pretended to kiss her father. Instead, she sucked his breath away until he died. Her next victim was her husband, whom she drained of blood as his harem of women watched, screaming. After that, the bride knew she loved the taste of blood, and she haunted Ireland for young male blood.

Now, once a year, the Dearg Due rises from her grave to seek a man. As beautiful in death, as she was in life, she finds a man, charms him to a closer relationship and drinks his blood. Is there a cure? Unlike Stoker's vampires, there seems to be no tradition of pointy-stakes or crosses to vanquish the Dearg Due. However, to keep her in her grave, at least temporarily, you could build a cairn over it. That helps for a while.

Sluagh

Please do not laugh at these strange creatures for they are dangerous. They were once humans like you and me, but they died as sinners and turned into the Sluagh. They seem to hover somewhere to the west of Ireland, waiting for somebody to die, then they gather in vast flocks in the sky and swoop down on the house where the soon-to-be-deceased is lying, clamouring at the doors and windows to enter.

Don't let them in, for the Sluagh are hoping to steal the soul of the recently dead. There are defences, of course. In old Ireland, people often kept closed any windows that faced west so the Sluagh could not enter. In modern Ireland, people tend to forget some of the old tales and old ways, so perhaps the Sluagh still gather, looking for their next victim. For the sake of the souls of the deceased, keep your western facing windows closed!

Carman

A nasty god-type creature, Carman was the Gaelic goddess of evil magic. She was not a nice person in any way. As the matriarch of her family, she had her sons Dub - darkness; Dother – evil and Dain - violence. When this charming family came together, they created havoc and horror for anybody and anything they came across.

However, she and her brood have now gone. The Tuatha

de Danann, the family of Danu, who was a much more benign goddess, countered their black magic with white magic, defeated them and sent them westward across the sea. More power to the Tuatha de Danaan!

I doubt Ireland will miss Carman and her sons.

NINE

BEWARE OF THE DOLOCHER

Now, this is a Dublin tale which deserves more than a passing reference. I must confess that I had never heard of the Dolocher until a gentleman in a Dublin pub asked me. 'Have you never heard of the Dolocher?'

'No,' I replied.

He gave a small, secretive smile. 'Well,' he said. 'Maybe you should.' Glancing suggestively at his half-empty glass, he continued. 'I could tell you if you like.'

I liked, of course, even although my thirsty companion seemed as if he would demand full payment for his trouble. As it was, I found the price worth paying, and between his story and other sources, I managed to piece together something of the legend. I am sure there is much more, but such is the way of legends: they grow legs with the passing years, and there is never a definitive source with a single, accurate story.

Back in the eighteenth century, people who could not pay their bills ended up in a debtor's prison, where they had to pay for their stay and still somehow raise the money to pay their debts. It was a cruel, strange way of doing things, but quite common, and Dublin was no exception. Dublin's debtor's prison was named The Black Dog – the same as Stevenson's character in *Treasure Island* – and was situated in Newhall Market, now Cornmarket. The more fortunate of the inmates could rent a bed for a shilling a night, a high price at the time. The less fortunate would spend the night in what was something like the Black Hole of Calcutta, made more malodorous by the public sewer that ran at its side, if beyond the prison walls. As well as debtors, the Black Dog also held prostitutes, so a fine mixture of those who lacked money and those who lacked morals, and often with a scoundrel in charge. One such scoundrel was the jailer John Hawkins who in 1729 appeared before the court on charges of corruption, cruelty and other related matters. All in all, it seems that the Black Dog was a place best avoided.

Sometime in the eighteenth century, an unpleasant man named Olocher found himself locked in the Black Dog. He was no mere debtor, but a man found guilty of the rape and murder of a girl and so condemned to death on Gallows Green. According to the legend, Olocher murdered the girl at the Liberties, a part of Dublin, according to my drinking buddy, 'sacred to all that is holy in the land of Ireland.' It is the home of Guinness, that darkest and arguably finest of Irish drinks.

However, Olocher escaped the hangman's noose by committing suicide, and his spirit is said to have haunted the place ever since. Given such a nasty man, it is not surprising that Olocher's spirit was also ugly. The first manifestation occurred a few nights after Olocher's death when one of the prison guards heard a strange noise coming from the cell in which Olocher had died. Surprised, as the cell was empty, he lifted his lantern and stepped closer, when something part-human and part-animal charged at him. Certain that the thing was a demon, the guard fled from the jail and collapsed. He was later found at the foot of some steps, unable to speak from shock. Only later did he explain what he had seen, a demon like a black pig. That was the first, but not the last, sighting of Olocher's spirit or, as it came to be known, the Olocher or Dolocher. Other guards now said they had seen something similar and the story grew in the telling.

Perhaps the terrified guard left the prison door open, or maybe spirits have the power to leave the jail in which they died, but the Dolocher began a reign of terror around Dublin similar to Burke and Hare in Edinburgh or Spring-heeled Jack in England. Things grew worse, according to legend, when the sentry at the front of the prison went missing. He was due to be relieved at midnight, but when his relief arrived, the man had vanished. The soldiers peered into the sentry-box to see nothing. They looked behind the box, wondering if he had fallen asleep there, and saw something that looked vaguely human. The soldiers stepped closer, gave a tentative poke – and found the missing man's musket, dressed in his uniform. The man had vanished, giving rise to the rumour that the Dolocher had eaten him and taken his soul to Hell. In eighteenth-century Dublin, where the Hell-fire club flourished, such stories were more than mere flights of fancy.

Only a few days after the sentry's disappearance, Dolocher reverted to his old ways and attacked an unfortunate woman outside Christ Church Cathedral, an area known as 'Hell' for the number of brothels, gambling houses and other places of low entertainment that existed there. This particular woman survived to report her attack to the concerned magistrates. She was in Christchurch Lane, she said, and the Dolocher lunged at her in the guise of a black pig, thrusting its tusks through her cloak and trying to rip her apart. Fortunately, the woman managed to discard her cloak, and she ran, escaping the Dolocher's grip. As usual with such creatures, the Dolocher targeted women. Bullies are like that; they prey on people they think are weaker than themselves; large countries attack smaller, gangs pick on people alone, big men bully physically weaker men, and insignificant men attack women or children. However, some women broke the supposed mould and fought back. One woman, heavy with child, was said to have beaten off the Dolocher but miscarried when she was safely home.

People said that the Dolocher was no longer human, but a devil, or a demon in the guise of a black pig. For the rest of that winter, the Dolocher ran riot in Dublin, attacking women, creating panic and making people scared to walk the streets. The people searched for him, with one band of lads gathering in a pub in Cook Street to fill themselves with Irish Courage before venturing forth to battle the pig-shaped demon. At length, suitable strengthened, and armed with an eclectic assortment of knives, old swords and anything that could stab, slash or cut, they sallied forth to kill any black pig they happened to meet, for they were sure that the Dolocher was a monster in pig's form. Perhaps they remembered that Christ took the demons from a man and placed them in a herd of swine, and had the vague idea that the Dolocher was something similar.

According to the legend, the band of pig-hunters did great slaughter along the streets of Dublin, killing every black pig they could, with the gentle women of the city encouraging the fun with statements such as, 'Oh, they have him now – them are the boys!' At that time, it seemed that pigs overran Dublin's streets, and the city's bailiffs helped the hunt with pikes. Despite the killing spree that filled the night with the squeals of terrified animals, next morning, there was not a dead pig anywhere. The streets were empty of corpses. Naturally, the superstitious believed that the bodies had gone the same way as the vanishing sentry.

With the coming of spring, the attacks seemed to fade away, or perhaps the pig-slaughterers had, in fact, killed the Dolocher. One wonders how much was mass hysteria and how many attacks by non-demons were attributed to the Dolocher. Summer was quiet and the good people of Dublin relaxed and returned to their regular peaceful pursuits of roistering, gambling, bear-baiting and the like. The boys with the blades had freed the city of the demon, they said. The hunters had ended the rampages of the hideous black pig; the Dolocher would no longer terrorise women and keep men inside the houses to irritate their wives. With winter, the Dolocher returned.

This season the creature concentrated on the area around Fisher's Alley and Christchurch Lane. The Dolocher robbed its first victim of a bundle of clothes, which seems a strange thing for a pig-demon to want, but the very idea of the return of the Dolocher created terror. However, the pig-demon's reign was about to end. Dublin was about to have a new hero.

In that age of horse-power and wheeled carts, men were used to long hours of manual labour. Among the strongest and most skilled of men were the blacksmiths, whose work with anvil, hammer and iron built muscles of steel. When one of these smiths visited central Dublin on business, he had mislaid his cloak so borrowed the cloak of his wife. Laughing at him, for the tight cloak made him appear a ridiculous figure, she placed her hat on his head in jest, for anyone less feminine than the blacksmith would be hard to find.

With the business part complete, the blacksmith's friends insisted he refresh himself in a local inn before he returned home. It was a wild night of sleeting rain and blustery wind,

JACK STRANGE

so the smith huddled into his wife's cloak, jammed her bonnet on his head and began to head back through the narrow streets. As he reached the area known as Hell, the Dolocher appeared, a black pig indeed with gleaming tusks, but tall as a man and snarling like the devil risen from Hell.

Perhaps the dark and rain disguised the blacksmith's size, or the Dolocher was confused, for it grabbed the smith and thrust him against the wall. That proved to be a massive mistake. Recovering from his initial surprise, the smith gave the Dolocher a single mighty punch that felled the creature to the ground, saying 'Be ye Dolocher, devil or what may, take that!'

When the Dolocher fell, the blacksmith gave it a hefty kick with his nailed boots and the Dolocher groaned and curled up.

'Halloo!' The blacksmith roared, with his voice echoing around the dark streets. 'Halloo! I've killed the Dolocher!'

On the blacksmith's words, a crowd gathered to see the vanquished Dolocher. They stood in a circle, staring and speculating until one, more daring than the rest, poked at the prone body. 'It's a man,' he said. 'It's a man in disguise!' Single-handed, the blacksmith lifted the Dolocher.

The black pigskin covering fell off at once, revealing the sentry who had vanished from his post the previous winter. As the man was still alive, the blacksmith carried him to the hospital at the Black Dog, where the jailers asked him what was to do? The one-time sentinel gave a full confession that surprised even the jailers; men used to the lowest of humanity and tales of anguish that would squeeze tears from MacGillycuddy's Reeks. Aware that he was too severely injured to live, the sentinel made a full confession.

He said that he had helped Olocher to commit suicide before his intended execution and a female friend of his had started the rumours of the devil-pig attacking people across the city. He also claimed to be involved in the pig slaughtering, where some confederate of his helped to remove the bodies to a cellar in Schoolhouse-lane, so giving the appearance of a supernatural agent at work. The culprit died the next day, having solved the mystery – or were the authorities not a little quick in accepting his tale? Perhaps they were only trying to calm the public down and hiding the reality of a half-demon stalking the streets of Dublin. Maybe the Dolocher still exists, waiting in the half-dark, searching for victims.

TEN

LEGENDS OF THE MOUNTAINS OF MOURNE

It is a well-known phrase 'Where the Mountains of Mourne sweep down to the sea', and these Ulster mountains are undoubtedly an impressive sight and as beautiful as any range anywhere. They are also immensely storied, with myths and strange legends that add depth to their appeal. There is only one warning, though. As well as the usual dangers of weather and wind that applies to every hill wander in Ireland, be careful of the Slieve Binnian light. This unearthly glow will try to guide the unwary away from the haunted copse at the Spelga Dam where a chieftain lies buried. Best let him rest in peace. Now that warning has been given, welcome to the hills.

The place names of Mourne are often a guide to mysteries and past events about which people have told stories. For example, there is Maggie's Leap, which is a gorge in a cliff-face with a dizzying drop below and the sea crashing against the rocks. Such a name begs the question, who was Maggie, and why would she, or anybody else, wish to leap across such a place? There are two theories about Maggie, (and probably more). The first story is a bit vague and claims that Maggie was a witch from the bad old days. The second is much more detailed and says that she was a local girl, the daughter of a poacher named Deegan.

As usual in such stories, Deegan the poacher was popular with the local people and less so with the authorities. He also taught Maggie the tricks of his trade and the lore of the hills so that she could wander the slopes or merge with the rocks as well as any four-footed denizen of the mountains. Not only was she proficient in hill-craft, but Maggie was as beautiful as it was possible to be, which made her an object of desire for the woman-starved soldiery who marched to and fro on the slopes of the hill in their continuing quest for poachers, smugglers and other ne'er-do-wells. As Deegan got older and slower, Maggie became ever more active in her activities until she became the prime poacher of the Mountains. Knowing how good she was, the soldiers redoubled their efforts to find her, but Maggie could elude their clumsy attempts on the hills while beguiling them with a swing of her hips or a flash of her eyes.

Now, there is another little dispute here, for, in another version of the tale, Maggie is no poacher at all, but a simple country girl who collects seagull eggs to eat. Such a practise was quite common in the old days when families ate whatever they could to survive. Anyway, Maggie was returning from a visit to the cliffs of Dundrum Bay with her basket full of eggs when half a dozen soldiers spotted her. For once, Maggie was at a disadvantage as the soldiers spread out to block her path. She tried to run, but with the cliff face at her back and the soldiers in front, her options were limited. The soldiers followed, laughing as they saw Maggie approach the great slice in the cliff. They knew she could not jump that; they had her now.

Glancing over her shoulder, Maggie saw the soldiers approaching, laughing, leering, shouting out obscenities. Maggie had a choice: Try and jump the chasm or face a fate worse than death. She jumped. As fit as a mountain goat and charged by desperation, Maggie soared across the gap to land safely on the far side and with every single egg in her basket unbroken. The soldiers could only stare, for none of them dared to try the chasm. And that is how Maggie's Leap gained its name. Others say that Maggie fell to her death, but I can't believe that. Not our Maggie.

Look also for Jenny Black's Hill near Warrenpoint. Many years ago, a witch named Jenny Black lived on his hill, or so the legend says. She may have lived here in the seventeenth century, when the persecution of witches and those believed to be witches, was at its height. According to the legend, she sat at her door with her spinning wheel and the obligatory black cat, spinning spells and cloth simultaneously. The stories claim that the cat spoke to Jenny when visitors were present, but in my experience, cats only do such things in private. They are far too smart to give themselves away to strangers. Jenny was not alone in her witchery, for the surrounding hills, the hills of Clonallon, were thickly wooded, and notoriously the haunt of all sorts of supernatural creatures, so that people avoided them at night time. Jenny, of course, used the bad reputation of the woods to her advantage as she turned herself into strange shapes to frighten travellers. There were tales of Jenny frightening horses and helping to murder a farmer by the name of O'Hare by lifting him and dropping him into a lough. There was also the usual tale of Jenny turning into a white hare, but in her case, she terrified dogs that were hare-coursing. Jenny put a spell on two boys who were with the dogs, taking them to a cave inside her hill. Once there, a witches' coven surrounded the boys, making them dance around a cauldron, into which they threw various herbs. After being made to dance with the witches, one of the boys touched one of the witches with a piece of witch hazel he happened to have with him. As everybody then knew, witch hazel neutralises the power of witches, and the witch the boy touched dissolved. The boy moved around the coven, touching each witch, so they also dissolved, allowing the boys to flee.

Jenny Black had other tricks in her broomstick. On Halloween, she gathered her coven together to cast their spells, causing the local people to counter the witches' evil by carrying candles through the dark woods of Clonallon in the hour before midnight. According to local folklore, if the candlelight remained steady, good would prevail, while if a wind blew out the flames, evil would win. Given that the 31st of October can be quite stormy, it sounds like a bit of a gamble to me.

Perhaps it is not surprising that the people grew a little fed up with Jenny Black. Gathering together, they hunted her down and burned her at the stake, and finished the job by burning down the whole evil forest of Clonallon. Nevertheless, if you happen to be passing Jenny Black's Hill, watch out for a white hare. It may be Jenny, coming back to get you.

Another captivating little spirit is the Blue Lady, who drifts through the Tollymore Forest Park. It is strange that she is blue when most female ghosts are green or white. The Blue Lady used to haunt Tollymore House until that house was demolished in the late 1940s and the Blue Lady became homeless. She is in good company, however, for many scenes from the series Game of Thrones were filmed in these woods.

Place names are fascinating. The modern ones, such as Draperstown in County Derry, tell of settlement patterns and planned villages, while others have evolved and can be thousands of years old. The names of rivers and loughs often retained their names while the people who lived around them moved. Waves of settlers, Mesolithic Neolithic, Celto-Ligurian, Celtic, came, hunted, farmed, bred and intermingled with the indigenous peoples or drove them away, but the original names for geographical features often remained. The later arrivals created their own stories to explain the names. Lough Shannagh in the Mournes is one such. The name is said to mean Lough of the Fox, and here is the story:

Back in the days of yore (in other words I don't know when) one of the local chiefs had a daughter named Sheelagh. Now, as we are all aware, women used to sit by the fireside, spinning wool, cooking for their men, obeying their husbands and counting the flying pigs. In reality, there was always a quota of women who were as wild and daring as any man, and Sheelagh was of that ilk.

Sheelagh was a noted hunter, riding her horse as she galloped across the slopes of the hills and over the fertile fields. On one occasion she was in the Mountains of Mourne chasing a fox with the menfolk of her clan clustered around her. As the hunt continued, Sheelagh pulled further ahead until she was away out in front, with the men labouring to catch her. Up on the mountains, the weather can change in a heartbeat and what started as a bright day soon altered as the mist rolled in. With the brush of the fox firmly in her sight, Sheelagh galloped on, following everywhere the fox ran. Even when it ran into a lough, Sheelagh was so intent on the hunt that she followed, shouting in excitement and with her horse splashing into deep water.

Losing sight of the fox under the water, Sheelagh realised that she was in difficulties and tried to find her way out. She could not and drowned there. Ever since, the lough has been Lough Shannagh, meaning Lough of the Fox.

Is that a true story? Is it a memory of some tragedy? I doubt we will ever know, but the Mountains of Mourne are like that, they are hills where truth and fiction wrap around each other to form an interwoven blanket of such depth and complexity that nothing seems inevitable except the beauty of the scenery and the stark bite of the wind.

Slightly inland from the mountains, the land is stunningly beautiful, with fertile farms, rolling countryside and more history per square mile than most entire countries can boast. It is a land of heroes, villains and religion, a landscape that has spawned a diverse range of people such as Catherine O'Hare, the mother of the first European child born west of the Canadian Rockies and Andrew George Scott, the infamous Captain Moonlight who caused havoc in the Australian outback. Perhaps more strangely, the same village that produced O'Hare and Captain Moonlight was also home to Patrick Brunty, a name that is hardly known except in Ulster and some literary circles.

The Brontes are among the most famous figures in English literature, with their Yorkshire background and tremendous writing skills. However, how many people know that they have a robust Irish heritage? The Bronte's father was Patrick Brunty, who began life as an unskilled and unlettered man in the little hilltop village of Rathfriland in County Down, a little inland from the Mountains of Mourne. The eldest of ten children, which was a pretty average number for the time, Patrick was born on the 17th of March, 1777, St Patrick's Day. After a patchy working career and a lot of self-improvement, he became a schoolmaster at the advanced age of sixteen. Recognising his potential, two local clergymen helped in his education, so Brunty entered Cambridge where, in 1802, he officially altered his name to Bronte. Academics seem to disagree why Patrick Brunty should wish to be Patrick Bronte, with some thinking he may have wanted to disguise his Irish background and others saying the new name was a tribute to his classical training in Cambridge. Brontes was the Greek word for thunder and the name of one of the Cyclops, a race of one-eyed giants who met Odysseus.

It is a bit strange to think that the Bronte sisters had their father's Irish accent when they were young. The local people ridiculed Patrick and the Bronte sisters for being immigrants, even though Patrick was the local clergymen and the sisters were born and bred in England. History has treated them more kindly, and now they are recognised for the literary talents they undoubtedly possessed. In Ireland, Rathfriland has not forgotten the Bronte legacy, with a Bronte Court in the village and a Bronte Heritage Trail in the surrounding countryside.

This chapter has only touched on the Mountains of Mourne and the surrounding area. The mythology, legends and stories run deep here, contributing to the strangeness.

ELEVEN

THE IRISH CURSE

I HAD NEVER THOUGHT of Ireland as a place where cursing was an art form. To my mind, a curse is only a curse, but while leafing through a nineteenth-century Irish newspaper, as is my wont, I came across this all-encompassing beauty.

To the man who wouldn't pay the Printer:
'May he be shod with lightning and
    compelled to wander over gunpowder
May he have sore eyes and a chestnut burr
    for an eye-tone
May every day of his life be more despotic
    than the Dey of Algiers
May he never be permitted to kiss a pretty
    woman
May he be bored to death by boarding school
    misses practising their first lessons in
    music, without the privilege of seeing his
    tormentors.

May his boots leak, his gun hang fire, and his
fishing-lines break.

May his coffee be sweetened with flies and
his tea-cup seasoned with spiders

May his cattle die of disease and the pigs
destroy his garden

May his shirts have no buttons, and his bed
be never aired

May a troop of printer's devils, lean, lank and
hungry, dog his heels every day, and a
regiment of cats caterwaul under his
window each night

May the famine-stricken ghosts of an editor's
baby haunt his slumbers and hiss 'murder'
in his dreaming ear

May his cows give sour milk and his churn
rancid butter

In short, may his business go to ruin and he
go to hell.'

THAT PIECE WAS from the *Cavan Observer* in 1860 and got
me thinking about Irish curses. Perhaps naively, I asked a
couple of people in my then-local public house in Dublin,
and they treated me to an excellent selection of curse words,
most of which, unfortunately, I already knew. They were no
different from the terms of abuse used freely in Scotland and
not entirely for what I was hoping. I had to research in more
academic arenas.

Ireland, like most other nations, has its quota of curses,
both in mythology and history. There are famous curses, such
as the ones in the old story of the Children of Lir where three
children were cursed by being turned into swans for
hundreds of years.

You will have heard of the ballet *Swan Lake*; you may even have watched it, but were you aware that there may be an Irish connection? The legend of the Children of Lir is ancient. Nobody knows quite how far back the story goes, but it is almost undoubtedly pre-Christian. When King Lir's wife died, he was left with four children and no woman to help him bring them up. The obvious choice for a new wife was Aoife, his late wife's sister. Aoife, however, had magical powers and turned the children into swans, with a lifespan of nine hundred years. The children were cursed to live for 300 years on Lake Derravaragh, the next three hundred at the Straits of Moyle and the final 300 on the island of Inish Glora. However, Aoife was not completely cruel; she allowed the children to retain their voices so they could sing away the years.

As usual, there are several versions of the story. One says that the children heard the bell of a saint or some other Christian, and the sound broke the spell. The children returned to themselves and returned to King Lir, who banished Aoife from the kingdom. That is an ancient curse, but it shows how powerful they could be.

Curses are intended to harm the victim, either physically, mentally or emotionally and often contain a form of magic. Sometimes curses happen when the victim strays into a spot owned by the fairies such a fairy fort, as raths are sometimes known, or damaging a fairy tree, a hawthorn. People could also inadvertently curse themselves by standing on a famine grave, the last resting place of somebody who died during one of the periodic famines that inflicted Ireland, particularly the Famine of the 1840s. Ireland seems to be a dangerous place to walk if one hopes to avoid a curse!

Often the person doing the cursing augmented the words with magic, using something belonging to the person he or she wished to curse, such as hair, nails or even a piece of clothing, and a magic wand or similar. Ireland is the only place I have been where there were even cursing stones.

On my tour of Irish pubs, I asked a few people if they knew any strange Irish curses, and noted down what they said. Disregarding those that I already knew as being common currency, and dismissing many that were colourful but obscene and therefore not suitable for a book that young eyes may read (sorry folks), I still found an excellent collection from various people. Thank you, Seamus, in the John Hewitt in Belfast, for your humour and help, and Monica for your often-racy input.

Many of the curses invoked the devil:

May the devil take your last penny.

May the devil make a ladder from your spine.

May you be burned and scorched. (Does this mean 'go to hell'? Seamus from the John Hewitt was adamant that it did.)

May you all go to hell and not have a drop of porter to quench your eternal thirst! (This curse combines eternal suffering with the Irish love of drink, although Seamus said that he has never heard this curse spoken.)

May you die without a priest (Another condemnation to go to hell, according to Seamus.)

May the devil break your bones.

May the devil make splinters of your legs.

May the curse of Mary Malone and her nine blind illegitimate children chase you so far over the hills of damnation that the Lord himself can't find you with a telescope.

May the devil blow you in the air.

May Hell's seventeen devils go after you with pitchforks and buckets of brimstone.

I curse you that the devil will turn the seat of your chair into a bed of red-hot metal and every pretty girl you meet into a sharp-tongued harridan. (That one was from a mild-looking lady in Waterford. She had laughing eyes, yet added details that would curl the hair of a sergeant of the Army Ranger Wing.)

May the lamb of God thrust his hoof through the floor of heaven and kick your arse down to hell.

There are other curses involving the devil, but the ones I give are a fair sample of an entire genre. Other curses invoked the fear of loneliness or of not belonging, which seemed a terrible fate in a country famed for its hospitality:

May you never have a hearth to call your own.

A widow's curse on you

God's curse on you

Bad ending upon you.

May the cat eat you, and the devil eat the cat (If the cat eats you, then you died alone with nobody to care what happens.)

May you be long astray. (Again, a lonely life.)

Other curses only involve bodily or emotional discomfort

May you get the itch and have no nails to scratch with.

May night always befall you.

May your bottom always be itching when you are in the church (thank you, Monica, although I'm sure you made that one up.)

Strife and stress upon you.

Weariness of heart be upon you.

May sorrow betide you.

That you may be a load for four before the year is out. (Four people carry a coffin, so that is a death curse.)

And finally, the simple curse of leaving a place or travel in danger

May you leave without returning.

That you may not come home safe

That you may never be heard of again

All in all, the Irish have quite a comprehensive collection of curses. My helpful advisors were pleased to provide me with the ones they knew, and I am sure they would be as happy to make up new curses, just for the pleasure of the game.

Some people, seemingly women, had, or possibly still have, the power to place a ritual curse on others. These women were usually on the lower social spectrum and cursed as a means of retaliating against some twist of fate or more often a person in authority who has acted unjustly. During the Famine of the 1840s and the evictions that followed people's inability to pay their rent, women were known to curse the landlord. However, such cursing was not without thought, or danger, since once issued, the curse must fall somewhere. If the landlord or his agent deserved the curse, then God's vengeance would strike him, but if not, then the curse may bounce back on the woman who uttered it. As curses are said to be the opposite of prayers, asking God to curse somebody may be the same as asking the devil to bless them, if the devil's blessing brings Bad, not Good. To follow that strange, twisted reasoning, that is possibly why black witches are said to recite the Lord's Prayer backwards. As some ancient rituals involved walking around a church or other holy site sunwise, east to west, then walking in the anti-sunwise, or anti-clockwise, would have the opposite effect, cursing rather than a blessing. That belief may be pre-Christian or ante-Christian for there is no mention of sunwise rotation in the Bible. Despite that, the early Irish holy men seemed very prepared to curse anybody who crossed their sacred path.

It was possibly the Druids, those elusive holy men about whom so much has been conjectured and so little known, who began the Irish love of cursing and words. According to legend and early stories, they were masters of the Word, the use of the right word to create Good and the wrong to wreak Evil; indeed, they were or may have been, magicians as powerful as any magi of the East. Their power lasted until they met the still more powerful Word of the Christian saints. One argument says that the Druids were the forerunners of the witches or of the wise women and men who knew the herbs of the countryside as well as having the ability to place charms and spells on people and animals. While some of these wise women and, less often, wise men, had their palms crossed with silver to curse people, others asked a similar remuneration for removing curses, so cursing was a cottage industry of its own accord in old Ireland.

I have mentioned that in Ireland, even a stone could be used to create a curse. The following little story concerns cursing stones.

There is a great deal of sadness in Irish history. There are massacres and famines, atrocities, murders and curses. Now, most curses are directed at individuals, but this is Ireland, which is a strange place at the best of times, and 1884 was anything but the best of times. This particular curse was aimed at an entire ship.

You may have heard one of the phrases 'send a gunboat' or 'gunboat diplomacy' which is often said to characterise British foreign, and sometimes domestic, policy during the heyday of Empire. The gunboats, which were at the sharp end of politicians' manoeuvrings, were built for endurance rather than speed. They were maids-of-all-work, able to sail up an African river to combat slave-traders, face Chinese pirate junks off Hong Kong or show the flag from Fiji to the Caribbean to support British interests. On occasion, they also helped the civil power in Ireland, on less savoury and decidedly unglamorous business.

HMS *Wasp* was one of these gunboats. A Banterer class composite screw gunboat, she was built by Barrow Iron Shipbuilding in Barrow in Furness, England, in 1880 and operated from Queenstown, now Cobh, for service in Irish waters. In 1883 she carried a cargo of seed potatoes to tiny Inishtrahull Island off Malin Head in County Donegal, where the population was close to starvation. To keep things in perspective, the Society of Friends donated the potatoes, rather than any government body. The following year HMS *Wasp* was sent back to the same island.

Lieutenant Nicholls was in command, sailing from Westport, County Mayo to Moville in Donegal. The crew would not be happy as *Wasp* was picking up bailiffs and police to evict three impoverished families from Inishtrahull for not paying their rent. Inishtrahull is and must always have been a bleak spot, stuck out on the wild Atlantic, now uninhabited and the most northerly point of the Irish Republic. It would be a hard place to live and grow crops, but families had called it home for generations, so eviction for them would be as traumatic as for anybody else.

As so often on the west coast of Ireland, the weather was unsettled, with banks of clouds, spattering rain and the odd Atlantic gale adding spice to the voyage. A couple of hours before dawn on the 22nd of September, 1884, *Wasp* sailed between Tory Island and the Donegal mainland. The lieutenant on watch was relatively inexperienced with these dangerous waters and just before four in the morning *Wasp* crunched onto a reef. She must have been sailing at some speed for the collision broke her back. She sank so quickly that there was no time to launch the lifeboats; she went down in fifteen minutes, taking fifty-two men with her. Only six survived, to be rescued by the islanders of Tory, nine miles off the coast of Donegal.

So much for history. Now for the myths and legends that add so much to the story. One concerns the lighthouse on Tory island: Was the light on or off when *Wasp* was close? There are rumours that the lighthouse keepers knew what Wasp's mission was and deliberately doused the light to hamper her. There is no doubt that the light was on after the shipwreck.

There is another story, which sceptics dismiss without thought. But sceptics tend to dismiss anything they don't understand, or which does not fit in with their often-narrow view of the world. Tory Island has a unique store of mysticism, from blessed clay to secret charms, and was home to what was known as cursing stones, *cloch na mallacht* or *cloch thorai*, which seemed to date from as far back as Neolithic times. These stones had been retained for perhaps thousands of years in their home within a saucer-shaped disc stone. The people of Tory thought the gunboat was going to evict families from their island and used the stones to lay a curse. Whether that story is true or false, the parish priest was reputed to have believed it. He took hold of the cursing stones and threw them, with their thousands of years of history, into the sea.

But we don't believe in cursing stones, do we? Not in this enlightened twenty-first century! Of course, we don't. A stone is just a stone. Now tell that to the queues of people who wait patiently, day after day, to kiss the Blarney Stone.

Although Tory Island has lost its cursing stone, it still retains its *Leac na Leannan*, the Wishing Stone, perched on the top of Balor's Fort. King Balor of the Evil Eye lived here in the days of the Formorians, and as the name Tory means bandit, then he was probably well suited to this windy place.

Who were the Formorians? Well, that question has intrigued historians and folklorists for some time. Professor Alfred Smyth in his book, *Warlords and Holy Men* calls them 'a sinister people ... who in the prehistoric past terrorised the coasts of the Gaelic world'.

Folklore credited Balor or Balar with having a single eye that destroyed everything it fell upon, so in its own way, it was a curse. Dun Bhaloir or Balor's Fort is on the eastern, slightly more sheltered side, as a peninsula with cliffs nearly 300 feet high. To reach the fort, the bold explorer must cross a windy isthmus. On the north is the Wishing Stone, with the legend that anybody who stands on this flat rock, or who even throws three stones onto it, receives a wish. Good luck!

However, the essence of the story is the power of the ancient curse. It is hard to reconcile the Royal Navy of the nineteenth century with a curse from Neolithic times, but the ship was well crewed, with an experienced crew and the officers knew the coast, yet still managed to run aground. One can believe or disbelieve, but nobody can argue with facts.

From the strange tale of the cursing stones, the next chapter will deal with another stone that is famous far outside Ireland's bounds.

TWELVE
KISSING THE STONE

So THERE I WAS, hanging upside down on the walls of an ancient Irish castle, with drizzling rain adding to my discomfort and a soft-spoken Irishman muttering quiet encouragement. Stretching to the utmost, I managed to manoeuvre myself in the correct position, puckered my lips and kissed that weeping chunk of stone people called the Blarney Stone.

I had done it! First, I had negotiated the five miles from Cork to Blarney and found the castle amid the glorious gardens, struggled up the 127 stone steps, and dragged, pulled, cajoled and shoved my reluctant wife up to bear witness to my bravery. Once I survived that minor ordeal, I had lain on my back and wriggled into position, warped my ancient spine, grabbed the useful steel railings, ignored the hellish drop beneath and accomplished the necessary.

Now I was undoubtedly blessed with the Blarney, the gift of the gab. No more would I stand tongue-tied in the corner while others held the floor. No more would I lose an argument to my quick-witted better half. I was now bound to be one of the most eloquent of speakers, able to talk myself out of awkward situations with charm and a smile.

'Is that it?' My less than impressed wife said when I righted myself.

'That's it,' was all I could think to say as my Irish guide smiled to me. Or possibly he was smiling at me.

'Good, you can buy me coffee now,' said the pragmatic one. 'You're too old for all those gyrations.' She was right, of course, again. I am far too old for such gyrations.

Now, you might ask yourself why I was hanging upside down kissing stones when there was a perfectly good wife on whom kisses would be more appreciated. Well, the answer is Irish. This chunk of rock was the famous Blarney stone, which must be one of the most storied stones in the world, and as such it comes well within the orbit of strangeness in this green island of Ireland.

The Blarney Stone is within the walls of Blarney Castle, which the MacCarthys built about the fifteenth or sixteenth century. Although time, weather and changing living conditions have ensured that the interior of the castle is a bleak shell, the external walls still stand as a reminder of the glory days.

Strangely enough, kissing the Blarney Stone to gain eloquence is a relatively modern concept, barely two centuries old. According to legend, the Blarney Stone grants more than the usual blagging with which sundry politicians hope to encourage their followers and bemuse their rivals. Instead, the Stone bestows the ability to persuade people with a blend of wit, skill and sometimes even a twist of truth. One of the greatest orators of the twentieth century was the British Prime Minister Sir Winston Churchill, who kissed the Blarney Stone in 1912. As Churchill's speeches inspired a nation and kept the fires of freedom burning through the darkest war years of 1940 and 1941, perhaps we can claim that this cold chunk of stone helped defeat the evils of Nazism?

There are many other stories wound around the stone, some stretching far back in time, others only a few centuries old.

Ireland being Ireland, there has to be at least one religious legend attached to everything. The Blarney Stone has a few such legends. According to an ancient story, the Old Testament prophet Jeremiah carried the stone with him when he travelled to Ireland. Jeremiah claimed that the stone was Jacob's Pillow. As any Biblical scholar will know, Jacob features in the Book of Genesis, where the Israeli patriarch slept at Bethel, using the stone as a pillow. As he slept, Jacob dreamed of angels and a ladder between Earth and Heaven and so consecrated the stone to God. When the stone arrived in Ireland, it became known as the *Lia Fail*, or the Stone of Destiny. Unknown hands placed this already mysterious stone on the Hill of Tara, perfectly positioned for the High Kings of Ireland to stand when receiving their crowns. I have scoured the Bible for any references to Jeremiah's visit to Ireland, but without success. It seems a long way to travel carrying a large chunk of stone, but perhaps a storm drove Jeremiah's ship to the far west.

Those of us, who know such things, will be aware that there is also a Stone of Destiny in Scotland, or perhaps two such stones. Another Irish legend states that when the English were invading Scotland. King Robert the First of Scotland made shifts to hide the Scottish Stone of Destiny. With English armies, backed by Scottish traitors, rampaging all over Scotland, Robert decided it might be better to send the Stone out of his kingdom. Accordingly, he sent it to Cormac McCarthy, King of Munster, for safe keeping. As

Cormac was the owner of Blarney Castle, he kept the stone there and possibly loaned King Robert some men to aid him in the War of Independence.

According to the story, after he had assured Scotland's independence by smashing various English invasions, King Robert thanked King Cormac for his help by breaking the Stone in two, with half remaining in Scotland, and a half in Blarney Castle. There may be more truth in that legend than is commonly realised, for although Edward Plantagenet of England claimed to have stolen the Stone from its home at Scone, when peace broke out, King Robert did not demand the return of the Stone. Why should he, when Edward had stolen a useless chunk of sandstone, and the genuine Stone had been squirrelled away in perfect safety in Blarney Castle?

Another religious tale attached to the Stone says that it's the very same stone that produced water when Moses struck it. I can vouch from personal experience that there is plenty of water where the Blarney Stone is presently situated, except that it comes from above rather than leaping from within. In saying that, I did not try the striking trick; I'll leave that to people blessed by God.

Yet another religious tale claims that the Blarney Stone is not the Stone of Destiny at all. A Crusader brought the Stone back from the Holy Land with the story that it was the Stone of Ezel, where David hid from Saul. The spiritual connection remains active.

One well-known story is based in the sixteenth century when Queen Elizabeth of England sent her armies to seize Ireland from the indigenous inhabitants. The Earl of Leicester rode to capture Blarney Castle from its proper owner, Cormac Teigue MacCarthy. Leicester no doubt believed that with the power of the English crown on his side, he should be able to persuade MacCarthy to part with Blarney without much difficulty. He was wrong. MacCarthy invited the earl to a series of banquets where he beguiled him with engaging words and smiles until Leicester gave up, knowing that MacCarthy outclassed him in polite conversation and pure Blarney. The result was that Blarney Castle, with its stone, remained with MacCarthy and the Virgin Queen used the word 'blarney' to describe a man clever with his tongue.

Despite all the legends linking the Stone with the Middle East, it is bluestone, the same as the rocks of Stonehenge, and it is native to Ireland. That scuppers the old Holy Land legends but all the better for that. Ireland's beauty, culture and history are every bit as interesting as anything in the Middle East.

Another of the Stone's origin legends is a little strange but perhaps more akin to Irish folklore. The MacCarthys were a royal family at a time when Ireland was divided into rival kingdoms, but there was a High King over all, with judges and courts to decide and dispense justice when kings fell out. It seems that one Cormac MacCarthy got himself into a legal dispute when he was building Blarney Castle. Now Cormac was a warrior, but he was not happy about appearing in front of learned judges and lawyers and others with talented, devious tongues, so he prayed for help to the Sidh, the fairies.

A beautiful lady named Cliodhna answered his prayers. Some said she was a queen of the fairies, and others insisted that she was the queen of the Banshees or the goddess of love and beauty, but Cliodhna might have been either, neither or all three. She was just herself and none the worse for that.

'How can I help you, Cormac?' Cliodhna asked with a smile that could charm the birds from the trees.

'I need an eloquent tongue to argue my case,' Cormac told her.

'Kiss the first stone you meet with on your journey to the court,' Cliodhna said, 'and you will win your case.'

Cormac walked away with his head down, not understanding, until he came to a considerable chunk of rock. However, he had asked for help and took Cliodhna's advice, landing a smacker on the cold stone. Immediately he did, he had the power of eloquence. His words spun a silver web around the courthouse so even the judge, old, learned and cynical in the ways of the world, was convinced. Cormac won his case. He was so impressed that he had the Stone lifted and built into his castle of Blarney.

Armed with this accumulation of knowledge, folklore, fiction and fun, I approached Blarney that wet summer's day. Of course, I asked for more information at the castle itself. The attendant at Blarney told me that a Crusader carried the Sone from Jerusalem, which fits in with one of my earlier legends, and added that it was part of an altar, which ties in with the Stone of Destiny story. However, he also said that the castle was built in 1446, long after the time of King Robert of Scotland and the Stone was built into the walls to stop the local clans from grabbing it for themselves.

Not long ago, as Ireland measures time, the method of stone-kissing was a bit more dramatic. The kisser was held upside down over the castle walls to kiss the stone. I mentioned that to my wife, who shook her head. 'I hope the women were wearing something decent under their skirts' she said severely. I nodded, of course, and did not mention the smile in her eyes. She was right, of course, but the image was intriguing.

Now here is another theory, one that warps around facts like an Irish storyteller weaving a tale over a pint of Guinness on a November night. The MacCarthy clan was influential in its day, kings of the area and proud men and women. As was the Gaelic tradition, the MacCarthys were also patrons of poetry, music and prose, with Blarney Castle, the home of a bardic school. This school survived the bloodshed when the English Queen Elizabeth brought her warfare to Ireland, to become a renowned centre of poets, famous throughout Ireland. It is possible that this combination of skill and art at a place already known for its legendary Stone began the tale that it was the Blarney Stone that gave the poets their expertise, and not the many years of hard work needed to become a Gaelic poet.

To me, that gives a touch of logic to the stories, although when we waited in the queue, the Dublin lady immediately in front assured us that one ancient King of Munster, possibly called Cormac (were these kings all called Cormac?) saved an older woman from drowning. She was a witch and cast a spell over the stone to give it the power of eloquence. So there is yet another tale to add to the Blarney list.

THIRTEEN
LEGENDS OF THE BURREN

I DID NOT EXPECT the Burren. I had read about it in advance, and people had warned me that it was like nowhere else in Ireland, but even so, the sheer strangeness of the place was astounding. As this little book is not intended to be a tourist guide, I won't fill the pages with facts, figures and statistics. I want to try and catch the atmosphere, which is as strange as anywhere I have ever visited.

The area known as the Burren is like a limestone plateau, scattered with archaeological and historical remnants and imbued with myths and legends. The name comes from the Gaelic word *boireann*, one meaning of which is 'stony place.' Within this stony place are also areas of surprising fertility, with bright wildflowers and Holy Wells as a reminder that God has not entirely forgotten this remote corner of Ireland. How the old people ever scraped a living here is a mystery, but they did, and animals still do, with wild goats, and dozens of birds including the intrusive cuckoo.

The Burren is in County Clare in the mid-west of Ireland, near villages with evocative and very Irish names such as Ballyvaghan, Kinvara and Lisdoonvarna, which is a small place with a big heart and a matchmaking festival that deserves a chapter all to itself. Amidst the near-lunar landscape of limestone clints and grikes, Lisdoonvarna has its very own Iron Age fort as well as waving palm trees that look slightly out of place in Ireland. Grikes, a helpful woman informed me, are spaces between the limestone pavements, often disguised by greenery, and a bit treacherous for the unwary walker.

The villages provide welcome watering places for the traveller here, while at least seventy megalithic tombs and other strange monuments enhance the landscape and are worth visiting. One of the must-see-sites is Poulnabrone, a dolmen whose name may mean 'The hole of the sorrows.' This place dates back to 2500 BC, and the chamber beneath the structure contained over twenty adult bodies, with six children and an unborn baby, together with grave goods including a polished stone axe, arrowheads and two quartz crystals, presumably treasures of the period. To us, in the supposedly sophisticated twenty-first century, this site is mysterious, strange and perhaps slightly unsettling. We can never know how the builders viewed Poulnabrone.

Another of the must-see sites in the Burren is the wedge tomb of Gleninsheen near the Caherconnell ring fort. The wedge tomb has a large slab supporting a stone roof and again dates from around 2500 BC, when this area must have been more densely populated than it is now. Not far away was found the Gleninsheen Collar, a gold gorget from about 700 BC, so 1800 years later than the tomb, arguing for long residency in the area. These sites might not sound strange, but when I visited them in their lonely landscape, they felt stranger than any ghost story. The thought that, over four thousand years ago, people were busily building here, on the extreme fringe of Europe, was actually breath-taking.

Later, much later, the Celts came to Ireland and the Corco Modhruadh clan owned or occupied the Burren. The name means 'people of Modhruadh.' With the usual Celtic genius for division, the Modhruadh split in two with the O'Conchubhair holding the west and the O'Lochlainn in the east.

Not surprisingly, a place with such a landscape and millennia of visual history also has a plethora of myths and folklore. Take the Blackhead at Galway Bay for instance. A Fir Bolg chieftain known as Irghus lived here in the old, old days. The Fir Bolg were the people who inhabited Ireland even before the Tuatha de Danaan, which makes them pretty early inhabitants. Long after Irghus came and left, a Banshee took up residence. This particular Banshee was known as Bronach the Sorrowful –are Banshees ever given cheerful names, like Bronach the Joyous or Bronach the Happy? – And she existed at the beginning of the fourteenth century. Bronach was an ugly Banshee and one that it was best to avoid. During these disturbed years, English, Scottish and Irish armies all marched around Ireland, and the local chief, Donchad O'Brien, led his men to the abbey of Corcomroe, where an enemy force was sheltering. As Donchad marched forward, he saw Bronach in all her primaeval ugliness. According to the story, Bronach had long grey hair, a crinkled forehead, bloodshot, savage eyes, a large blue nose and a beard. So Bronach was not quite a contender for Miss Ireland 1317.

When Donchad saw her, Bronach was at the edge of Lough Rask, washing a gruesome collection of legs, arms and heads, so the lough was as much blood as water, while human brains and hair floated on top. 'This will be your fate,' Bronach said, 'and the fate of all your men.'

'Not if we kill you first,' one of the warriors said, drawing his sword, but Bronach screamed, flew into the sky and vanished. Despite Bronach's warning, Donchad and his men marched to battle, where their enemies slaughtered them all at the battle of Lough Rask. Not the happiest of stories, but one well-suited to the Burren back in 1317.

A second legend concerns a monk named Colman whose brother was King Gaire the Hospitable of Hy Fiachrach Aidhne, or Gort as it is more commonly known. This minor kingdom is supposed to have been founded by the Fir Bolg, but more likely it was Celtic. In the seventh century, it was common practice for Celtic monks to find an isolated spot to pray, fast and meditate, and many sailed to remote islands off the west coast. However, Colman preferred the bleakness of the Burren, finding a quiet spot in there to spend Lent. After a while, hunger began to gnaw, and his companions asked Colman to pray for some sustenance. He did so, and within minutes a few minutes a string of dishes holding excellent food floated towards them followed closely by a troop of angry warriors. At once, Colman worked out what had happened: God had answered his prayers by taking the food from his brother's Easter table and sending it across the Burren.

All that remained was to deal with the sword-wielding warriors. Being a man of deep faith, Colman knelt to pray and was not surprised when the Lord responded immediately. The warriors and their horses found they could no longer move. The horses' hooves and the feet of the men were stuck to the ground, leaving Colman time to enjoy his meal. From that day forth, the route from Gort to the Burren was called the *Bothar na Mass*, the Road of Dishes.

One of the strangest Burren legends concerns a black-smith known as Lon Mac Liomtha. This gentleman was of the Tuatha de Danann and is said to be the first Smith in Ireland to make an edged weapon. He lived in a cave on the mountain of Slieve na Glaise. So far, there is little strange about Lon, except that he made up for having only one leg by the addition of an extra hand in the middle of his chest. Lon found this third hand useful for holding the iron on his anvil while he hopped on his single leg.

Nobody knows how old Lon was, except that he had been in Ireland for many years. They did comment that he was friendly with a cow though. This animal, Glas Gaibh-neach, lived on the slopes of Lon's mountain, Sliabh na Glaise. Lon had brought the cow to Ireland from Spain and treated her with great affection. Glas was also a bit different from other cows for, when milked, she could fill any container of any size. To cut a very long myth short, two women bet that Ireland did not have a bowl large enough to hold the milk from Glas, one milked the cow into a sieve, and the result was seven rivulets that still flow.

The legends and my words do not do the Burren justice. The strangeness is in the place itself, the strange rock forma-tions, the hiss of the wind, the views, and the crash of the sea all combining to create something indescribable. Words cannot describe it. One has to visit.

At the end of the Burren are the Cliffs of Moher. The name sounds like something out of Tolkien, and there is a story that these dramatic cliffs influenced that writer as he attempted to create English folklore with his Lord of the Rings masterpiece. Of course, Ireland does not need any author, even a genius like Tolkien, to make up myths, legends and folklore for there is plenty to go around.

The Cliffs of Moher in County Clare have such an abundance of strange stories that the trouble is knowing what to leave out, rather than searching for material to put in. I will start with the story of Hag's Head, a rock formation at the southern tip of the cliffs. People once gave the name 'Hag' to old women, or sometimes to witches, so already we are verging on the mythical. As the name suggests, the imaginative may think that, when seen from the north, this formation looks like a woman's head, staring out to sea.

In the dim past, about two thousand years ago, when the iron legions of Rome were struggling to keep down the Britons and failing to subdue the Caledonians beyond the Wall of Hadrian, Ireland remained free. It was the time of heroes, and none more so than Cu Chulainn, a warrior of the Red Branch, the iron shield of the King of Ulster. However, even heroes have their weaknesses, and Cu Chulainn preferred to avoid a woman named Mal, a famous witch who fancied him for a husband, or at least a bedmate. According to the story, Mal chased Cu Chulainn up and down the island of Ireland until he reached Loop Head in County Clare. From Loop Head, Cu Chulainn seemed to have nowhere to go except out to sea or into Mal's willing if witchy hands, but being the hero that he was, he found another way out. Jumping onto the sea stacks, he leapt from stack to stack, with Mal a few steps behind. Fortunately, Cu Chulainn reached safety, while Mal slipped and fell, landing in the sea, and that's how Malbay got its name. When Mal plunged into the water, the surrounding rocks formed into the shape of her face and earned their title of Hag's Head. Or so some people say.

As well as witches from long ago, there were other creatures here. Mermaids are not generally associated with Ireland, which is strange as there are nearly two thousand miles of coastline and a strong Norse influence. It seems to be the case that mermaid tales came with the Norsemen and remained, often tinted with the mythology of the indigenous peoples. In that case, the mermaid of the Cliffs of Moher should have an Irish slant. Read this little tale and decide.

Many years ago, a man was fishing at the base of the Cliffs of Moher when he saw a mermaid lying on a rock, quite close by. Naturally intrigued, he began to talk to her, all the while watching the magic cloak that all Irish mermaids had. Unable to prevent himself, the man darted forward, snatched the cloak and fled to his nearby home.

Without her cloak, the poor mermaid could not return to the sea, so she ran to the thief's house and searched for the cloak. The man had hidden it so well that the mermaid could not find it. When the mermaid pleaded, the thief said that he would only return the cloak if the mermaid agreed to marry him. Grief struck, the mermaid married the thief, and with time bore him a daughter and a son. As the years passed, the man grew careless and one day left the mermaid alone in the house while he went out fishing. This time the mermaid found her cloak, put it on and returned to her natural element, never to see the thief or their children again.

That was it, no drama, nothing but a sad little tale with a happy ending, but other water-borne creatures were not as friendly as the mermaid. There was a specific eel, for instance. This eel crawled out of the sea and made its home in the cemetery beside the small village of Liscannor, where it lived by feeding off the corpses. Another account calls this a giant eel that attacked and killed the locals. Now, people were upset at the thought of their loved ones, either dead or alive, ending up in the stomach of an eel, so a saint by the name of Macreehy killed the eel and now the entire parish is named Kilmacreehy. That may seem a bland little story, but it is based on the carving of an eel that once existed in Kilmacreehy until wind and weather wore it away.

If mermaids, eels and brave warriors are insufficient to keep the visitor's interest, a lost underwater city might do the trick. There are many names for this mysterious Irish city, including Kilstpheen, Cill Stuithin, Cill Stuifin, and Kilstu-itheen, although the most commonly used name is Kilstiffen. As always with such places, there are several similar legends. The central theme seems to be that there was once a pros-perous city here, but when the king lost the golden key that opened the castle doors, or more likely the gates that kept the sea at bay, the city sank beneath the waves. Only when some-body finds the key, will the city surface again. At present, Kilstiffen is said to be off Spanish Point, somewhere. The key may be in a lough on a mountain-top, or under a gravestone on Slieve Callan.

While some people have said the city is still beneath the waves, and visible on a clear day, others say it is deeply submerged. Every seven years, Kilstiffen rises and then sinks again. According to one legend, if anybody sees the city when it's above water, that person will die before it appears again, so best not look too hard.

How accurate is this legend? There is probably not a submerged city of gold, but at the reef of Lisacannor Bay, ancient forest land has been flooded, which may be the basis for the story. It may also be a memory of Hy Brasil. However, there is a similar story of a submerged country off Cardigan Bay in Wales. Perhaps the legends are linked and once, many centuries ago, there was land here, engulfed by a giant flood beyond the memory of humanity, Maybe, sometime, some-body will write a book that tells of this flood, and perhaps of a handful of survivors who built a boat and told the story...

Another fabled spot on these cliffs is the Leap of the

Foals. When St Patrick crossed the Irish Sea with his words of a new, peaceful religion, the Tuatha De Danaan, the Gods who had lived in Ireland for many centuries were not happy at all. According to a strange legend, rather than fight a battle they knew they would lose, they transformed into horses, galloped into Kilcornan and hid in the darkness of the caves. Many years later, seven horses crept out. Blinded by the now – unfamiliar sunlight, they galloped along the cliffs but fell over the edge at Aill Na Searrach, the Cliff of the Foals. Does this little story show the death of paganism before the light of Christianity?

None of these tales can capture the glory and raw power of these cliffs. They are like a full stop to the island of Ireland, a final gesture of defiance before the land ends and the mighty Atlantic Ocean begins. The Visitor Centre here is worth an hour or two of anybody's time, with its Atlantic Edge Exhibition.

Overall, the Burren and the Cliffs of Moher form a strange, nearly magical place that has to be visited.

FOURTEEN

LEGENDS OF THE BOYNE

FAMED in history for the 1690 battle, the River Boyne is said to take its name from Boann, a Danann goddess whose name means white cow. She was the daughter of Delbaeth, and although she was married to the handsome Elcmar, she cheated on him with the Dagda, one of the major gods at the time. Boann seems to have been rather a wayward wife, for when Elcmar asked her not to seek knowledge from Connla's Well, she did so anyway. Of course, women in old Ireland were always free-spirited, much like women in Ireland are today.

Otherwise known as the Well of Wisdom, Connla's Well is the source of the River Shannon. At Connla's Well, nine enchanted hazel trees hung over the water, periodically dropping nuts for Fingar, the one-eyed salmon of wisdom to eat. When Boann travelled to the well to find knowledge, either to eat the hazelnuts of wisdom or the salmon that consumed them, she did a strange thing. Boann walked widdershins, counter-sunwise around the standing stones and lifted the stone that covered the well. This tribute to the dark side forced the well-water to surge upwards. There are two versions of what happened next. Either the water caught Boann and took her over the land and out to sea, or she ran, and the water followed, with the route of her running becoming the course of the River Boyne.

At one time the Boyne was known as Bealach na Bo Finne, which apparently means the Path of the Bright White Cow. I do not think that name is a personal reference to Boann.

Unfortunately, the tale of the founding of the Boyne may not be entirely accurate. For a start, Boann has links with three gods, any one of which could have been her husband. Her lover, however, was the Dagda, and her son was Angus Og, whose story comes later. Angus became the god of poetry, youth and love. According to modern geographers, the Boyne has its source at Trinity Well in County Kildare. Not as exciting as the mythological beginning but possibly more accurate.

Whatever its origin, the Boyne is one of Ireland's most storied rivers, and that is a massive claim in an island where there are legends in every village and tales in every town. It is in the north of the island and stretches, or rather winds, for seventy miles through Leinster. The course of the Boyne takes it past some fascinating places including Tara, Tlachtga, the site of the Battle of the Boyne, Trim Castle, the temples at Newgrange, Dowth and Knowth, Navan and the Hill of Slane.

The Battle of the Boyne is famous in legend, with the Protestant King William defeating the smaller army of the Catholic King James. Both claimed the throne of Scotland and England (a united crown since 1603) and by association, Ireland. The battle was fought on the 1st of July, 1690, although a later alteration of the calendar means the corresponding date today is the 12th of July. Both monarchs had various titles, with King James being James VII of Scotland and II of England, while William was William II of Scotland and III of England and just happened to be the nephew of James. Things are already a little strange, are they not? While William was a noted supporter of Protestantism, one of his major allies was the Spanish Empire, devoutly Catholic and where the Inquisition was in full swing. Although the battle was fought in Ireland, with Dutch, Scottish, English, Danish, Polish, Norwegian, German, Irish and French troops, the future of Ireland was only a side issue.

The reality was a war to contain French expansion, with William, a significant player as the French king, Louis XIV pressed toward his Dutch lands. In saying that, William also had French Protestants on his side, oh, yes, and the Pope also supported William, and the mainly Catholic Austrians, while some of William's best soldiers, the Dutch Blue Guard, were Catholic.

So this fight between the supposedly Protestant army of King Billy and the supposedly Catholic forces of King Jim was nothing like the legend would have us wish. That fact is especially true as the ruling class of Ireland mainly supported James, despite being Protestant. The folk group The Dubliners used to sing a song *The Sea Around Us* with the lines: 'If the Irish had sense they'd drown both in the Boyne' and given the amount of blood spilt by two non-Irish poten-tates fighting to rule Ireland, and a succession of others before them, I would have to agree.

As well as bitter memories of the battle, James VII and II left a ghost for he is said to haunt nearby Athcarne Castle. The story goes that he slept here the night before the battle, which is plausible as he actually owned the place. The castle is also said to on a burial cairn that is thousands of years old and has other ghosts including a blood-stained young woman and a soldier hanging from a tree.

Another of the places the Boyne passes is Tlachtga, the Hill of Ward at Athboy. It is not much of a hill in terms of height, but it has an impressive history and the remains of 2000-year-old earthworks that themselves are on a much older site. According to legend, the hill is named after Tlacht-gla, the daughter of Mogh Ruith, a druid who had triplets, died and was buried here. Tlachtga was the site of the cere-mony of Samhain, the fire festival to signal the start of winter that is now best remembered as Halloween.

Not far from the Boyne is Kildemock, which has the only 'jumping church' in the world, or at least the only one of which I have ever heard. Kildemock is in the middle of Louth, beside Ardee. The remains of Millockstown Church sit on a hill, so God and the churchgoers can enjoy the view of the distant hills. Unfortunately, when I was there a blanket of rain obscured the view so I can only say what people assured me was correct. Only one of the church's walls jumped, and that was nearly three hundred years ago, but people are still wondering what made it happen. This strange little ruin stands amid glorious (if damp) countryside, with a legend that in 1715, the church wall moved of its own accord to ensure that the grave of an excommunicated man remained outside. Sounds strange? Well, it is. The church wall moved three feet from its foundations without any apparent cause.

According to my local guide, a young man with a serious expression on his face as he related the story, the church was ancient when it shifted, and a person of immoral standing, 'either a man or a woman,' my young guide told me solemnly, was buried within the gable. Shocked at having a sinner inside its walls, the church leapt across the grave so to keep its sanctity.

Although my guide was unsure, it seems that the immoral person was a man, ironically a stonemason, who shifted his faith from Catholic to Protestant, thus making him locally unpopular. He died when he fell as he was working on Stabannon Church, and his family buried him within the church at Kildemock. On the night of his burial, the wall jumped, leaving his grave outside.

If you don't believe the church jumped itself, try to think of another reason why a wall could move. Did a storm push it? I've never heard of a storm shifting a wall yet leaving it virtually undamaged. However, that is the official explanation. The wall is no skimpy modern thing but a substantial chunk of masonry, some nineteen feet in height and three feet wide. It would take an Atlantic hurricane to push that weight and bulk three feet across the ground, let alone an Irish gale. Now, that is an extraordinary church.

Not too far away are the Loughcrew Cairns. Although Ireland has a fantastic collection of strange mythology, she does not need to create stories for places such as this, as the reality is sufficiently astounding. The truth is literally out of this world so I'll give a rapid sketch. These cairns contain passage tombs replete with utterly fascinating carved artwork that stretches back literally thousands of years, to as far as 3,500 BC. Yet the symbols are not mere artistry; many indicate astronomical symbols while the ceiling stone of Cairn T, as somebody has unimaginatively termed the place, could be a star map, and apparently, at the time of the spring equinox the dawn sun fully illuminates this stone. Indeed, these Neolithic people were knowledgeable, highly intelligent and, to judge by the work, very skilled in stonework.

These cairns are near Oldcastle in Meath, a group of

small cairns, known collectively as *Sliabh na Calliagh* which translates as Mountain of the Witch. For once mythology and folklore are less colourful than reality, for the story says that a giant witch once stalked across this area, carrying an apron full of stones. Every so often, the stones slipped from her apron, forming the mounds or cairns. The witch was called Gatavogue, or *An Cailleach Bheara* (Bheara the witch.) There is a possibility that Bheara could be a garbled form of Bui, the Celtic Moon goddesses, which could argue that the Celts worked out the lunar and astronomical meaning of this place.

The Hill of Slane is another site near the Boyne that boasts an impressive past, imbued with mythology. Although only five hundred odd feet high, this hill still manages to impress, even without the obligatory religious connection. On this hill, St Patrick lit the first paschal fire in Ireland in 433 AD. That may not sound very interesting, yet it was a direct challenge to Leoghaire, the local king who had already set a fire on Tara for the pagan celebration of the spring equinox.

The story states that St Patrick sailed from the west coast of Britain, either Wales or Strathclyde in Scotland, and came ashore at Colpe in the estuary of the River Boyne. He and his men marched inland and that evening came to Ferts fer Feic, which translates as the Burial Place of the men of Fiacc. Most authorities think this mysterious burial site is the Hill of Slane.

King Leoghaire had ordered that nobody else light a fire, so he was furious when he saw Patrick's Easter fire on the Hill of Slane. Immediately he saw the flames; he ordered that somebody should extinguish Patrick's Christian fire.

St Patrick watched as men ran up the hill and threw water onto his fire. He might have smiled as the Christian fire remained burning. The pagans tried to pull the burning logs apart and stomp the flames into nothingness. Patrick's fire continued to burn. In fact, nothing the pagans did could extinguish Patrick's flame of Christianity, which is possibly the moral of that strange little story. In time, Patrick appointed a man named Erc as the first Christian bishop in the area, and later still a monastery was built here, the ruins of which still survive. Nevertheless, some academics doubt the veracity of the story, saying that Knowth or Newgrange were both more prominent and therefore the more likely site for Patrick's Easter fire.

Even before the arrival of St Paddy, the Hill of Slane had its spiritual side, for there was a Healing Well here that the Tuatha de Danaan used to doctor any wounds they received in battle. Not only that, but a Fir Bolg king by the name of Slainte was buried here and there is a burial mound on the hill to prove it. These early battles were brutal affairs, as this ninth century piece about the Battle of Magh Mucraimhe, fought some thousands of years before, makes clear:

Bitter sights were seen there – the white fog of chalk and lime going up to the clouds from the shields and targes... the gushing and shedding of blood and gore from the limbs of the champions and the sides of the warriors.

Very much later, in the seventh century AD, a Prince Dagobert arrived in Ireland from a small Merovingian kingdom called Austrasie, now part of France. Living in exile, Dagobert grew up at Slane and Tara. He is said to have married an Irish princess and returned to the take over the throne of Austrasia. If only partially true, this story puts Tara in its context as a European kingdom at a time of fluid national boundaries. There were a couple of kings named Dagobert of Austrasia, with one dying in 639 AD and another ruling until 679.

For a people who are renowned for having the gift of the

gab, the Irish are surprisingly quiet about the archaeological treasures of their island. Perhaps that is because there are so many of them, each one with its own strange stories and legends attached.

If Tara gets the praise and the fame, the group of tombs known as *Bru na Boinne,* is older. The name Bru na Boinne could mean 'the palace by the Boyne', or less poetically, 'the bend in the River Boyne'. These passage graves stand not far from the site of the 1690 Battle of the Boyne – for Irish history is multi-layered, with site on site and incident overlapping incident. The best known is known as Newgrange, and rose here before Egypt's pyramids were built. The incredibly skilful building has lasted well over four thousand years and is aligned to the Winter Solstice. Many people believe these people of the far past were ignorant barbarians, while instead they had an immense knowledge of the stars and could build structures that have outlasted anything we create today. Naturally, such an ancient piece of architecture has attracted much attention over the centuries, with tales and legends growing up. Three of these tombs, Dowth, Knowth and Newgrange itself, rise close to the banks of the Boyne and are far more impressive than the squabbles of silly self-important kings.

As in so many of Ireland's legends, the stories reach back to pre-history. Newgrange was said to be the home of Aengus Og, and the gods of the Tuatha de Danann. These gods were pre-Celtic, or so the stories say, and the quality and variety of the Irish stories would put the ancient Greeks to shame. According to the legend, Aengus' father was Dagda, and his mother was Boann, the Boyne's river goddess. When it was evident that Boann was with child, Dagda was a little annoyed and used her power to stop the sun until Boann conceived, so nobody knew what had happened. So for nine months, time seemed to stop, and Aengus was conceived and born within one day, which was so strange that he became Aengus (or Angus) Og, which means Young Angus. He was a tricky sort of god, and when Dagda told him he would have no inheritance, Angus asked humbly if he could at least live in Newgrange for a day and a night. When his father agreed, Angus told him that a day and a night meant all days and all nights, so he now owned Newgrange. Perhaps he had already kissed the Blarney Stone, to persuade a god with such ease.

Now Angus was a normal, healthy young god, and he had a notion to find himself a wife. At night he dreamt of the perfect girl for him, a young lady known as Caer. Angus wanted that young woman and no other, so he searched the length and breadth of Ireland to find her. Eventually, he succeeded, but Caer was a prisoner, sitting in chains with another hundred and fifty girls. When Angus found out that every second year, on Samhain, the first of November, Caer and her fellow prisoners become swans for a year, he determined to find and marry her then. He learned that if he managed to identify her from the other swans, they could be together. Being an intelligent sort of God, Angus found his Caer among the herd of swans on the water and swam out to her. However, the instant he placed a hand on her, he also became a swan. Happy together, Angus and Caer flew to the River Boyne beside Newgrange, where they can still be seen and sometimes heard, singing to the people who live in the ancient tomb.

Nearby Dowth does not have such a happy history. The name itself means darkness or the place of darkness, and it is the least visited and arguably least popular of the magnificent tombs beside the Boyne. The legends attached to this still-huge and immensely impressive passage grave are dark indeed, which makes one wonder why it should attract such gloom when other nearby tombs have brighter stories.

In common with the other tombs in the Boyne Valley, Dowth was created in the Neolithic period, by a community of people who lived by agriculture. Although it may pale in comparison with Newgrange, the fifty-foot-high Dowth has its unique charm and is worth a visit. Once it was more substantial, but nineteenth-century archaeology tended to destroy what the diggers should have retained. Even so, what remains is impressive, with decorated stonework that suggests the importance of the sun in contemporary religion, a theme highlighted by the positioning of the passageways to allow in sunlight at the winter solstice. Although much is known, in many ways even the most learned of scholars are groping in the dark at Dowth, although they are aware that it was a sacred site for upwards of three thousand years even before the Celts arrived. The Norsemen, of course, had no interest in such things and desecrated the sites in their search for loot. In the eighteenth century, it temporarily reverted to a religious use when the Roman Catholic then-owner, Viscount Netterville, built a strange structure on top so he could kneel in prayer on a Sunday morning. A servant was at Mass in the nearby Catholic Church and communicated the various stages of the service to Netterville, so he could retain his faith while keeping within the then anti-Catholic laws of Ireland.

All very interesting, you may say, with a yawn, but Jack is meant to be giving strange tales, not turning into a dry-as-dust historian. So here is the legend of Dowth, which dates from sometime before the eleventh century and probably a great deal earlier. At some time in the Dark Ages, a disease struck the cattle of Ireland, killing them by the hundred. Now, to a pastoral society whose wealth was in cattle, such an event was a catastrophe. Eventually, the disease became so bad that only one bull and seven cows survived in the whole of Ireland.

Shocked at the devastation, Bressal, the High King issued a decree from Tara and ordered that people carry his word to every corner of his kingdom. Every man in Ireland was to collect in a single place to build a tall tower to try and end the plague while there was still some hope. As the Irish poem says, the king made the tower:

> In the likeness of Nimrod's tower,
> So that from it he might pass to heaven,

The king's sister just happened to be a druid and said she could stop the sun to give the men more time to build the tower. The idea was sound, if perhaps unfair to the men who had to do the work, and the tower was making splendid progress until the lust of the king broke the spell.

The sister was a beautiful woman, so despite their sibling bonds, the king took her aside and made love to her. Naturally, that terrible sin broke the spell, and the sun resumed its progress. The men thankfully stopped work and the tower, the tomb, never climbed another inch. As a poet wrote:

> From that day forth the hill remains
> Without addition to its height:
> It shall not grow greater from this time
>   onward
> Till the Doom of destruction and judgment.

The coming of night gave the tomb its name of Dowth, the place of darkness.

The third of the three tombs is Knowth, which is not much different in size from Newgrange, and has two long passages inside, the smaller of which is more than thirty-six yards long. At one time Knowth was called Cnogba, which is said to come from Cnoc Bui, with cnoc meaning a hill, so the tomb was the Hill of Bui. Some people may ask who Bui was, well, she was the moon goddess or the hag goddess, and according to the story, Knowth or Cnogba sits on top of her. Other sources say that Bui was also known as Buach, and was the wife of Lugh Lamfhada, the High King of the Danann and the God of Lightning. There is an alternative theory that Bui was the daughter of Donn, Lord of the Dead, one of the Milesians, the Gaels themselves. Whoever or whatever she was, Bui was undoubtedly an important personage in her time, a goddess.

Leaving aside the gods and goddesses, Knowth is a must-see for its superb artwork, as it contains a quarter of all the megalithic art so far uncovered in Western Europe. According to the archaeologists, the passages of Knowth align to the moon, while some of the carvings on the kerbstones could signify lunar events, which tie in with the ancient story of the mound carrying the name of the moon goddess.

Thousands of years after Knowth was created, Iron Age people used it as a centrepiece for a ditch and later still the area was the capital of the Dark Age and early mediaeval kingdom of Brega. These people, possibly Celts, Milesians, Gaels, call them what you wish, evidently recognised the importance of the site. It is still fascinating today, which, given the sheer age of the place, is more than impressive.

Finally, I will mention Telxon, between Kells and Navan, mainly because it is a bit different. Once again, this area has incredibly ancient roots and this time an annual sporting festival that could even predate the original Greek Olympics. Teltown, more properly Tailteann, was the site of the Lugh-nasa Assembly, which was one of the quarterly feasts held in pagan times. This particular feast started on the first of August and legend claims it was to celebrate Tailtiu, the foster mother of Lug of the Long Arm and the wife of a king of the Fir Bolg who died on that day. Tailtiu was buried at Tailteann, giving the place its name, and her last request was for men to cut down the trees, creating space for her funeral games.

The three-day-event was open to anybody from any quarter of Ireland and lasted until 1168. The festival was revived after Irish independence and held in Dublin's Croke Park, but it faded away once more, which is a pity. In this age of globalisation, local events should be encouraged before the whole world becomes a single monoculture without variety or individuality. The island of Ireland, thank goodness, has a sufficiency of originality to make it stand out from the crowd, and the banks of the Boyne serve to illustrate what Ireland has to offer. The next chapter highlights another site near the Boyne, arguably the most important of them all.

FIFTEEN

THE HILL OF KINGS

WHAT CAN I say about the Hill of Tara that has not been told by a thousand writers and ten thousand visitors? Probably very little, yet I will try. Tara is unique. It is unique both in history and prehistory, unique in the hearts of Irishmen and Irishwomen and especially in the atmosphere. I have never been to a place where there are so many layers of history so densely packed together. Tara is a must. Tara, in a sense, is the soul of Ireland, more so than Dublin or Belfast or anywhere else I have visited in my perambulations around the island.

Yet when I first saw this hill of kings, I was disappointed. I did not know quite what to expect, but I think I hoped for something more outwardly dramatic. Instead, from a distance, it seemed little more than a slight rise amidst pastoral rolling and charming countryside. There was no immediate physical drama, only little tea shops and a straggle of visitors, some merely curious, some searching for something beyond their immediate ken, others wide-eyed, open-minded and grasping at the flavour of the wind and the feel of Ireland.

It was then that I found it. This place is about feelings as much as it is about history. It is the combination of the two that creates something intangible, and once you find it, you never, ever, wish to let it go. The location and history of Tara combine to create something that wraps itself around anybody who is susceptible to atmosphere, enters them and remains, long, long after they have left. Although I seek the strange, Tara goes beyond strangeness into a most relaxed sense of belonging. It is ethereal as if one has come home to a place one once knew, or one's ancestors once knew well. Tara is beyond my capacity to describe; the closest I have come to it is when I stood on the sands at Iona, or within the walls of Jerusalem. I can only say, come with openness and allow Tara to enter you. Do not try to understand this ethereal place. Only let it into your heart.

So, that's sufficient about my feelings for Tara and time to add my piece about the place itself. Ancient Ireland was divided into several small kingdoms, with a single High King over all, and as far as historians and archaeologists can tell, the Hill of Tara was from where the High King ruled from around the first century AD until the Norman-English invaded in the twelfth century. That in itself, a thousand years of continual importance for Tara, is impressive enough, but only the tip of a deep historical barrel.

The Hill of Tara has nearly thirty monuments on and around it, each one of historical and archaeological impor-tance, each one of special fascination. We shall start with the Rath of the Synods, purely because of the name. A rath is a circular enclosure, with a wall of earth, usually covered in turf. The Rath of the Synods has a mound within the rath, and at the turn of the nineteenth and twentieth century, when amateur and semi-professional archaeology was rampant, a group known as the British Israel Association of London excavated this site, convinced that the ancient Jews had hidden the Ark of the Covenant inside. The British Israel Association was strange enough without the Tara connection; for they believed that the Anglo-Saxons were descended from the lost twelfth tribe of Israel. As the Angles and Saxons were both German tribes and immigrated into Britain from north-western Europe, that particular idea is highly unlikely, but let's not allow historical reality to interfere with a good dose of strangeness. The British Israelis also believed that Britain should rule the world, which at a time when the British Empire was vast and still expanding, seemed a little more likely than it does now.

Not surprisingly, the British Israelis did not find the Ark, only a handful of Roman coins that might have been loot from a raid on Britannia. However, the expedition with its pseudo-science and hopeful digging on such an iconic site jangled a few nerves and had the authorities and Irish nationalists on edge for a while. With phrases such as the 'great Irish-Hebraic-cryptogrammic hieroglyph' to play with and a search for a connection with the ever-fascinating Freemasons, famous figures hastened to Tara to protest at this desecration. Arthur Griffith, the writer who helped found Sinn Fein, was only one of a distinguished bunch that included William Yeats, the writer and Douglas Hyde, later the first President of Ireland. They managed to ignore the armed guard as they registered their disapproval.

Maud Gonne MacBride, the suffragette and actress, did her part by standing on Tara to sing the Irish nationalist hymn *A Nation Once Again*, which did nothing to endear her to the authorities, to whom the idea of an independent Ireland was anathema. Her singing was particularly offensive to the landlord; a man named Briscoe, who had organised a party and a bonfire to celebrate the coronation of King Edward the somethingth, and instead had to listen to an Irish song. The entire episode was a clash of cultures and political ideas, where Ireland met Britain, Nationalism met Colonialism and science met amateurism on the Hill of Tara. In its way, it foreshadowed some of the events of the twentieth century. The idea of the British Israelis that Tara was the spiritual birthplace of the Anglo-Saxons was utterly strange of course, but that merits its inclusion in this book. Although nothing physical came of this excavation, the episode helped bring Tara back to the national consciousness of Ireland and possibly, in a small way to the attention of people in Britain as well.

In a way, that strange episode epitomises Tara. It is a place where ideas coalesce, a meeting of the spiritual and the practical. The Irish High Kings were crowned here, and, according to legend, druids did whatever druids were meant to do. The name Tara comes from Teamhair na Ri, the hill of the kings, which makes sense. In old Celtic society, the king had more than merely physical power; he also acted as a link between this world and the supernatural, a belief carried on into Christianity with the anointing of kings and the divine right of kingship.

The archaeology stretches back to around 4000 BC, so nobody is sure exactly what did happen here, although there is no doubt the site had tremendous importance. According to legend, Tara had associations with the Celtic god Lub and the goddess Medb, two deities with whom it was better to agree than to disagree. In some manner, Tara was a gateway to the Underworld or spiritual world, which would fit in with the apparent link between kings and divinity.

As well as the Rath of the Synods there is the Lia Fail, the famous Stone of Destiny, the coronation stone on which Ireland's High Kings was crowned (unless the Stone is at Blarney Castle of course.) Being Scottish, and accustomed to hearing of the Stone of Destiny being in Scotland, I was slightly surprised to hear the Irish version of the story. I will relate it here, or my version of it gathered from a variety of sources, and I apologise to any purists who may see things from a different angle.

The Lia Fail surmounts the Kings Seat at Tara, and one version of the legend says that it shouts out three times when the rightful High King touches it with hand or sword. The Tuatha de Danann, the ancient people from whom the goddess Danu was named, first brought the sacred stone to Tara, many centuries ago. Other legends say it was Jacob's Pillow, a story I have already mentioned under Blarney. The Stone has another, sombre purpose for it also marks the mass grave of some hundreds of Irishmen who rose against British rule in 1798. These United Irishmen fought a battle here against a well-organised British force and died under the fire of cannon and disciplined musketry.

Possibly older than the Stone of Destiny is the Mound of Hostages which dates to approximately 2,500 BC. The name is of later date and may come from the Celtic practise of kings taking hostages from their rivals to ensure there was peace between them. However, the mound is far older than any historical king and covers a passage grave, although it is always possible that Tara's kings used the area to hold prisoners.

Tara is slowly revealing her secrets, as geophysical surveys have discovered a henge beneath the surface. A henge is a Neolithic earthwork with a ditch within a bank. They are not uncommon, although Stonehenge in England is undoubtedly the best known because of the stone structures.

The henge at Tara is, or was, of wood, with over 300 wooden posts and with a diameter of over 170 yards, was much larger than Stonehenge. This henge surrounded most of the significant monuments on the surface of Tara, and its purpose is unclear.

St Patrick visited Tara in the fifth century on his mission to convert the pagan Irish to Christianity. According to legend, he met and converted High King Laoire here, so that king was possibly the first Irish Christian – Patrick was British, from either Wales or Strathclyde.

Overall there are more than thirty ancient monuments on Tara, or that the visitor can see from the hill, with others below ground. Around the area are the Neolithic memories of Uisneach, Four Knocks and Loughcrew, each fascinating in its own right. On the hill itself, or right beside it, is Finn's Well, Mound of the Cow, the Pinnacle Well, Rath of the Cow and other sites.

Two of the more neglected stones stand in the churchyard. One is said to show Cernunnos, the pre-Christian Celtic god of fertility, which is a strange thing to find in a Christian churchyard, but this is Ireland, home of weird things and unusual legends. Even the experts can't seem to agree about the date. It may be Neolithic, like so much around here, or Bronze Age. One monument that time has removed is the Cross of Adamnan, who was a sixth-century churchman who passed laws to protect the 'innocent' – women and children - from the worst effects of war. He tried to exclude non-combatants from indulging in battle in a move so far ahead of its time it was breathtaking. But Tara can grip you like that.

Possibly because of its historical and religious significance, fighting men have gathered here before embarking on expeditions to free Ireland from foreign foes, although their presence has not detracted from the overall ambience. The 1798 battle is a sad reminder that war is always more sordid than glorious.

Another theory is that Tara was the ancient capital of Atlantis, with Ireland the site of that mythical land. As Atlantis was supposed to have sunk under the sea, that is an extraordinary belief, for Ireland is still here (I say 'here' rather than 'there' as I initially wrote this piece while sitting on Tara itself, with a sheaf of notes to my left, and a transparent sheet sheltering my paper from a soft, grey rain.)

From first to last, 142 Kings have been associated with Tara, and if legends are to be believed, the hill must have seen some splendid sights. The stories claim that candidates for the High Kingship had to arrive in their chariots and drive them at some speed toward two standing stones that stood close together. When the stones recognised the rightful king, they would part, and the High King could drive to Tara. All other candidates would either turn away or crash into the stones.

Once he had undergone the official ceremony, the High King could stand on Tara and appreciate the significance of the view. I know I did, without the benefit of royalty. As I said, I was not overly- impressed when first I saw Tara, a rise on the landscape with a church and a few grassy humps on top, but once one takes time to look around, one can appreciate the site. An alternative meaning of the name is 'a place of great prospect', and nobody can argue with that; half of Ireland seems to be visible in a panorama of green, tree or bush-lined fields and distant hills. My timetable allowed for half a day on Tara. I arrived at seven in the morning, and I reluctantly left at ten that night, having experienced and enjoyed the changeable Irish weather. I could have stayed longer. I did not ever wish to leave.

It is only a few weeks since I left Tara, and already I have a longing to be back, a feeling that I left part of me behind on that sacred hill. It is nothing like I have experienced before and is vaguely unsettling, like Tara itself. It is as if I stepped out of another dimension to which I already long to return.

SIXTEEN
WHERE IS HY BRASIL?

In the last chapter, I mentioned the legend that Ireland was Atlantis. This chapter will begin with the story of another exotic island in the Atlantic, for the Irish people have always been aware that there was something to the west of them. Sometimes they thought of this green island as something mystical, an island of the fairies or the land of the dead. At other times they had a practical certainty that it was a place as solid as Ireland itself. The Dark Age Celtic monks were intrepid seafarers, venturing far beyond their coasts to discover the Faroe Islands and Iceland long before the Norse. An Irish monk named Dicuil, who wrote *World Geography* in 825 knew a Celtic holy man who had spent time on the Faroes and described Iceland, which he called Thule. Even before these holy explorers set out in their leather boats, a seventh-century Irish script says: 'There are three times fifty distant islands in the ocean to the west of us; each one of them is twice or three times larger than Ireland.' One of these vaguely suspected islands was long known as Hy-Brasil.

Anybody with even a rudimentary grasp of geography is aware that Brazil is a vast country in South America. It has nothing to do with Ireland, has it? Well, perhaps it has, in an indirect way.

There is an ancient legend about an island off Ireland in which lived a man with the title of Breasal, the High King of the World. This island was known as Hy Brazil or Hy Brasil, although there are other spellings. When the old-time saints voyaged westward to search for somewhere suitably isolated to contemplate God, at least a couple of them, St Brendan and St Barrind claimed to have landed on Hy Brazil. They named it the Promised Land. The island featured in Irish myths, but mythology merged with geographical exploration when, in 1325, a Genoese cartographer created a map that showed Hy Brazil in the sea west of Ireland. Other map-makers may have followed Dalorto in placing Hy Brazil off Ireland, or perhaps they used local knowledge. The cartographers typically placed the island off Galway Bay, a few thousand miles from present-day Brazil. That was also where a Catalan map put the island of Brasil, only twelve miles before Columbus sailed west. One wonders if Columbus used any of these maps when he sailed westward to find China if indeed that was his real objective.

Ships sailed from Bristol to find this mysterious island, with some thinking that the New Found Land of Cabot was Hy Brasil. In 1500 the explorer, Pedro Alvares Cabral, found a stretch of coastline in what is now known as South America. In time this land became known as Brazil: was there a connection with the old Irish legend?

Alas for legend and conspiracy theories; no, there was not. Cabral seems to have named this new land Ilha de Vera Cruz, or the Island of the True Cross. Later, the area became

Terra de Santa Cruz or land of the Holy Cross. It was not for some years that the name Brazil became attached. Despite the similarity of names, the South American Brazil has no connection with the Irish Hy Brasil. Brazil seems to come from brazilwood, which itself is named after *brasa* or ember because it has a red colour. The only connection between the two Brasils is on the national flag of Brazil, which contains a circle divided by a semi-circular channel, which was the recognised shape of Hy-Brasil.

Has the mythical Hy-Brasil ever been seen in more modern times? Strangely enough, it has. As recently as 1674, a Captain John Nisbet from Killybegs in Donegal was sailing west of Ireland when fog descended, blotting all visibility. Knowing how treacherous these waters could be, Nisbet sent men to look out for hazards as he waited for the fog to lift. When it did, Nisbet saw a series of sharp-fanged rocks, far too close for safety. He hove to in three fathoms, dropped anchor and sent a boatload of men to investigate the island that should not be there. While Nisbet fretted on the ship, his crewmen met an old man on the island, who gave them silver and gold. After that, with the weather moderating, Nisbet sailed away.

That was not the last time somebody saw Hy Brasil. In 1872, the author T. J. Westropp reported seeing Hy Brasil appear. It did not remain long, and nobody has claimed to have seen it since.

Of course, it is possible that Hy Brasil is one of these unusual mobile islands that seem to grace the Celtic nations of the west. In July 1878, the people of Ballycotton in County Cork saw an unknown island just offshore. It was no rough rock but a fully-fledged island with hills and forests. Ballycotton was a maritime settlement, so half a dozen fishermen set out to explore. They were experienced mariners, well used to landing on islands, but as soon as they neared this new place, the island disappeared.

Was this Hy-Brasil, which was said to appear one day every seven years? Or was it a mirage? Was Hy-Brasil always a mirage, a trick of the mind? After all, there is no miracle in mirages. They appear in deserts and at sea, and often when driving along a dry road, a motorist may see what she or he thinks is a pool of water in a dip of the road in front. If Hy Brasil was only a mirage, it is not alone, for the Irish coast, particularly on the north, has been notorious for such occurrences.

In September 1860, a strange mirage-like apparition appeared above Quigley's Point in Donegal. A family from Cardonagh were walking in the neighbourhood, and all stopped to stare in astonishment. In the sky to the north, they saw a line of ships maybe five miles long, sailing east to west. Not only that, but the ships were sailing down a high-banked river. As the family watched, more details became apparent. Some of the ships were moored to a fortress that was on top of a rock, while the vision was so clear that even the children of the family saw sailors hauling on ropes. The family stared at the image for at least half an hour before it faded away.

It was obviously a mirage rather than a heavenly visitation, but of what? The picture seems to correspond to a war fought a century before, when a British fleet sailed up the steep-sided St Lawrence River to besiege Quebec, a fortress on top of a rock. The British fleet formed a long column upriver before anchoring, with busy sailors as well as soldiers.

Such strange visions were once reasonably common along the northern shores of Ireland, with the Giant's Causeway and other parts of the Antrim coast being especially blessed. Another striking image arrived around 1848 when a group of fishermen were out on the waters of Loch

Foyle. They were returning home with the dawn when the clouds above parted to reveal an area of bright, clear sky. As the fishermen watched, an army appeared hundreds, then thousands strong. They marched across the sky, regiment after regiment, with officers leading their men, and then after some two hours, the clouds closed in and concealed this heavenly army. Was that a vision of events in Europe, then convulsed with a series of national revolutions where armies marched and counter-marched?

Overall, the images of Hy-Brasil may be explained as mirages, as other images seem to be. However, the accounts of seamen landing on such places have no such ready explanation. Were these seamen lying, or only confused as to their locality? Or was there some other, less rational explanation and these seamen landed on some land that people have not yet rediscovered, such as Atlantis?

I will finish this chapter with a short piece which has no rational explanation. In Celtic Ireland, Clonmacnoise in County Offaly was a major Christian monastic site, with a European-wide reputation for scholarship and piety. In 749 AD the *Annals of Ulster* reported 'ships with their crews were seen in the air above Clonmacnoise.' A later mediaeval account gives more details, saying that the monks were holding a meeting when a ship sailed over them. The crew of the vessel saw the meeting and dropped anchor, which the priests grabbed. One of the crew swam down to free the anchor, so the priests grabbed him too.

'For god's sake let me go,' the man said, 'for you are drowning me.' When the monks released him, the man lifted his anchor and swam back to his ship.

Was that another mirage? If so, it was not an isolated incident for there were other similar occurrences in Ireland including at the Teltown fair in 956, when a crewman also came down from the ship, was held and said he was drowning. A similar incident happened around 763 at the same location. Indeed, the two events were so alike that I suspect the later was a retelling of the earlier. Was there a single root for these stories? I will leave that to better scholars than me to work out.

SEVENTEEN
THE IRISH WAKE

IF THERE IS one tradition for which the Irish are well known, then that is the Irish wake. The image is well known, the gathering of friends and relatives to say farewell to the departed, the telling of stories as the whiskey, poteen –illegally distilled alcohol - and Guinness are passed around, the singing, sometimes arguing and always celebrating the life of one who is no longer there. A wake was a vital celebration that bridged the abyss between life and death and ensured that they remembered the departed in the best way possible. There is also a possibility that a wake was an attempt to avoid any premature burial.

Wakes are perhaps less common now than they once were, for the old wakes were a thing apart, something uniquely Irish with their mixture of Christian and (arguably) pagan customs. What they did do, was reinforce the conviviality of Irish life and strengthen the links of family that may stretch back to the days of the Irish clans. A hundred years or more ago, the womenfolk of the family and friends would prepare the body by washing it clean, often with holy water, and laying it out on top of a bed or somewhere similar in the best or largest room the house had to offer. The corpse may have been covered in crisp white linen and decorated with ribbons of white or black. The family bought candles and arrayed them around the body, partly as lights to guide the angels in, and partly to allow the dead to see her or his way to heaven. If the deceased were a man, the family would place a clay pipe beside his bed, and whatever the gender, the family placed tobacco and snuff around the room. With the theory that tobacco smoke hid the deceased from the devil, every man who visited the house had to light up. That particular tradition cannot be ancient, as tobacco was not introduced into Ireland, or indeed into Europe, until the sixteenth century.

With the dead ready in the room, often with a rosary around his or her hands, a woman remained at the side of the body until the pallbearers carried the coffin to the graveyard. The body was often placed beside an open window, to allow the soul to depart and make its way to heaven. Closing the window was forbidden, and if anybody closed the window, they would be cursed.

Only when the body was ready for burial was it considered safe to begin the keening, or crying. There was a reason for this tradition, for if the keening began before the womenfolk had prepared the body, the distinctive noise would attract evil spirits who could fly away with the soul of the deceased. This aspect of mourning was carefully orchestrated, with a woman known as the *Caointhe*, meaning the chief keener, being first to keen, and others following. The Caointhe did more than merely keen; she also recited poetry, which had been a Celtic tradition for the dead for centuries. Only the women keened for the dead, and to hear a houseful of women mourning at the same time was something to raise the hairs on the back of one's head.

This tradition stretched back for centuries, if not longer. In a fifteenth century account of the death of Cu Chulainn, Eimher, his wife took his disembodied head, 'began to bewail and lament over him, and began to kiss his lips and drink his blood.'

Other traditions may also seem a little strange, with towels or sheets placed over any mirror, curtains pulled shut, and clocks stopped at the time of the death. Being Irish, the mourners would ensure a plentiful supply of drink, with food there as a reserve. Food and drink were necessary as a full-blown wake could last three nights, or more, with women and men exchanging anecdotes about the deceased and laughing together as they played games in a manner too pagan for the church to approve. During the wake, the dead and the still living united in mourning, song and celebration.

Nobody seems to know where and when the Irish wake began. Presumably, it had some religious connotation although there is a vague tradition that the three days of mourning was to allow the deceased to recover if he or she was not actually dead but only in a catatonic state. There is also a possibility that those left behind were celebrating that their relative was entering the afterlife.

Although not associated with the wake, there would be more wailing at the funeral. Sometimes a Banshee would appear at the graveside and add its hideous scream to the wails of the mourners. The Banshee has always been a sign of bad luck, so her presence at a funeral allowed those present to be aware of their own mortality. One version of the Banshee legends claims that she only mourns the females of the family.

It is a pity that wakes are less popular – if that is the

correct word. They were a tradition that showed the uniqueness of the Irish people and must have helped ease away some of the grief that death inevitably brings. The next chapter is entirely different as it tells the story of one of Ireland's most strange women.

EIGHTEEN
RED MARY MACMAHON

DURING HER LONG HISTORY, Ireland has produced more than her share of interesting women. One of the most fascinating is Mary MacMahon, otherwise known as Maire Rua or Red Mary, a woman with red hair and a plurality of husbands, and a woman it was better not to cross.

Mary lived in the seventeenth century, one of the most turbulent times in even Ireland's rumbustious history. She may have been born in 1615 and made her mark on Ireland, and on anybody who happened to cross her path. Mary's first husband was Daniel O'Neylan, whose death left her a moderately rich woman. In 1639 Red Mary married again, and she and her new husband, Conor O'Brien, lived in Leamaneh Castle in the Burren area of County Clare, only a short half hour from the 200-metre-high Cliffs of Moher.

Mary was notorious for her bad temper and cruelty, and according to the stories, she would hang servants from the castle windows for trivial reasons. While men were hanged by the neck, women were hanged by the hair of their head, which would mean a lingering and agonising death. Legend also accredited Red Mary with slicing off the breasts of her maids if they did not come up to scratch. She must have had a very efficient Human Resources section to recruit more staff after such incidents.

Conor seemed to have been the love of Mary's life, and he was a hard man himself. According to legend, he prevented the local people from passing along the road from Burren that wound through his property. However, the Burren folk were not the kind to submit tamely, and a group smashed open Conor's gate and made him promise free access.

When she was not torturing her domestic help, Mary liked to ride her black stallion around the local countryside. This stallion may have been the same animal as a famous blind horse that terrorised her grooms. Mary was an accomplished horsewoman and boasted that no man could control her steed. Naturally, such a statement was only a challenge so many men mounted the stallion, which, according to folklore, was trained to gallop to the Cliffs of Moher and then throw the unfortunate rider over into the seething waves below. Mary did like her little jokes.

Mary also liked her men. She liked lots of men if the stories are accurate. As well as Conor O'Brien, she married at least two others and possibly as many as twenty or more. Her favourite husband seems to have been Conor, who fought against Cromwell's General Ireton. Legend says that Red Mary fought at Conor's side as he led fast, hard-hitting troops of horse to harass the invaders. On one occasion, Conor rode without Mary and came back to the castle, so severely wounded that Mary thought he was dead. In one version of the tale, Conor had been so effective in fighting that General Ireton gave five picked men orders to assassinate him. One of the five succeeded in shooting the Irish patriot. As Conor's men carried him back to the castle, Mary leaned over the tower, unmoved by the sight.

'What use have I for a dead man?' She called.

Finding out that Conor was still alive, Mary turned nurse and did her best for him, only for Conor to die in his own bed. Not a woman to let a slight go unavenged, Mary caught the Cromwellian who had shot her husband and strung him up from a tree, or perhaps a window of her castle. She then ordered her sons to surrender to Cromwell's men. If they entered Cromwell's peace, they should be able to retain their lands. If they resisted, they would nearly inevitably be defeated and probably killed by what was perhaps the most efficient and ruthless army in Europe.

Conor's death left Mary a wealthy woman, but vulnerable to Cromwell's avaricious soldiery. Pragmatic to a fault, Mary chose her most elegant clothes, jumped in her coach and six and rode to Limerick to find another husband, a man who would ensure she retained possession of Leamaneh Castle. Given the political climate of the time, that meant a Cromwellian soldier. At that time, General Ireton was besieging Limerick, with his army camped outside the town. A sentry stopped Red Mary, pointing his pike at her and demanding to know who she was and what her business was in Limerick.

Never a woman to be intimidated by a mere man, Mary responded with loud shouts, making so much racket that General Ireton himself emerged from his tent to see the reason for all the noise.

'Who are you?' Ireton asked.

Red Mary replied with a classic one-liner. 'I was Conor O'Brien's wife yesterday, and his widow to-day.'

The words may have taken Ireton aback. 'He fought us yesterday.' Ireton said. 'How can you prove he is dead?'

Mary glanced over the assembled faces. 'I'll marry any of your officers that ask me.'

With her red hair, bright clothing, elegant bearing and broad lands, Mary must have appeared a splendid catch so a Captain John Cooper at once proposed. Now that she had secured her next husband; Mary knew that her son, Donat, would fall heir to the castle.

During her life, Mary was reputed to have given birth to twelve children, and with Conor's wealth held in her hands, she turned the castle into a splendid mansion, pleasing to the eye despite the cruelties carried on behind the façade. As with most marriages, there is no knowing what went on behind the closed doors of Leamaneh Castle, but Cooper and Mary seemed to jog along together. However, Cooper grew careless, and one morning, while shaving, he argued with Mary and insulted her beloved Conor. Red Mary took instant offence, leapt from her bed and gave Cooper such a mighty kick that he later died. So that was the third husband out of the way. Other versions say she threw Cooper out of the bedroom window or made him ride her stallion to the Cliffs.

Either way, Mary needed another man, and possibly another after that. According to the legends, she amassed the amazing, and probably apocryphal, total of twenty-five husbands. One version of Mary's legend says that she married most of her later husbands for one year and a day, after which they divorced. That sounds like a legal Handfasting rather than a genuine marriage, so there may be some truth in the legend. Perhaps Mary was trying out the men to find one she thought suitable for her. There is another twist to the story, claiming that Mary sent her servants into the houses of her husbands, and when she divorced them, she kept their property, so expanding her lands and wealth.

Again, according to legend, Red Mary's death was as

grisly as her life and, as usual, there is more than one version. The simple variant claims that her tenants grew tired of her cruelties, tied her to a tree and left her to die of starvation and exposure. The more picturesque version claims that her tenants threw her into the trunk of a hollow tree, sealed her in and left her there. Yet another version says she was not killed at Leamaneh Castle at all, but at the Druids Altar at Carnelly, near Clare Castle.

Red Mary has no known grave, yet her spirit remains inside Leamaneh Castle, and a red-haired ghost endlessly patrols the rooms, corridors and the grounds outside. Sometimes her harsh laughter can be heard.

So much for legend. Is there any truth in the stories?

Leamaneh castle exists, with the old walls derelict now but gardens and courtyards outside to remind of the splendour in which Mary once lived. Red Mary was a real person, although the tales attached to her have grown in the telling. Red-haired Mary and Conor O'Brien did fight the Cromwellians, until 1651, when the invaders killed Conor at the Pass of Inchicronan. Mary next married John Cooper, a cornet rather than a captain. Cooper left the army, speculated in land and amassed a small fortune, although he later lost both his money and the castle. There is no evidence that Mary killed him in any of the picturesque ways legend claims.

In 1664 King Charles II gave Mary a royal pardon on murder charges relating to her efforts during Cromwell's wars. She may be buried at Coad Church in Kilnaboy, beside her two daughters. May she rest in peace as I, for one, would not care to wake her.

The next chapter will look at a couple of strange incidents involving less dangerous Irishwomen.

NINETEEN

CAN THE DEAD REAPPEAR?

This chapter will look at a couple of cases where the dead appeared to the living. In one case the departed crossed oceans, in the other, it was in response to a pre-arranged meeting. Nobody has solved either strange mystery.

The Irish diaspora started in the sixteenth century with wandering soldiers and increased as famine, oppression and poverty forced women and men from their homeland to all corners of the world. One of the places the Irish settled was Tasmania, that magical island to the south of the Australian mainland. Many had no wish to go there, being sent as convicts or political prisoners in the late eighteenth and nineteenth centuries. However, by the late nineteenth century, such transportation had ended, and visitors and residents appreciated Tasmania for its beauty.

In early 1888 an Irish lady named Miss Hervey was in Tasmania on an extended visit, staying with one of the more affluent ladies of the island. One evening in April as she was descending the stairs inside the house, she met her cousin climbing in the opposite direction. Now Miss Hervey was a level-headed lady, and she knew that her cousin was in Dublin, many thousands of miles away so could not be in Tasmania. This image she saw must have been something else. Either on the advice of her host, or because she thought the sighting was bizarre, Miss Hervey wrote down what she had seen, and the time.

Her note ran something like this: 'On the 21st of April, 1888, at 8 in the evening, I saw a vision of my cousin in a faded grey dress.' Folding up the note, she placed it somewhere safe and tried to forget all about the incident. It was not until June, two months later, that Miss Hervey learned that her cousin had died of typhus in a Dublin hospital at the exact time she had seen her. Not only that, but the grey dress she wore matched the uniforms of the nurses in the hospital. No explanation was possible, except that her cousin had come to Tasmania to inform her she had died.

The second incident is much more detailed; in fact, it is suspiciously well known, but still strangely compelling. This story was first recorded in the eighteenth century by the granddaughter of Lady Beresford, the main protagonist. Lady Beresford was born as Nichola Sophia Hamilton while her foster-brother John Le Poer later became Lord Tyrone. The parents of both children died far too young. At a time when most people were either religious or pretended to be so, Nichola's guardian was an atheist and tried his best to bring up both children to be disbelievers. However, the h children were firm in their Christianity and, possibly to spite their atheist guardian, they made a strange promise to each other to prove the existence of a life hereafter. They promised that the first to die would appear to the other, so showing the atheists wrong.

In time the foster siblings grew up and married. Nichola married Sir Tristam Beresford and became Lady Beresford.

John became Lord Tyrone but died young and, as he had promised, he appeared beside Nichola's bed.

I do not know how Nichola reacted as her dead foster-brother appeared at her side. Presumably, she was surprised, even shocked, but she listened as John revealed her future life to her. Nichola learned that Sir Tristram would die and she would marry again and have four children. That news may or may not have been welcome, but when John mentioned that she would die on her 47th birthday, Nichola became scared. With the fear came disbelief, and Nichola demanded to know if she was dreaming or if John had really returned from the dead.

As if to prove his existence, John took hold of Nichola's wrist. She must have gasped in pain, or at least shock as her wrist immediately withered. And then John vanished. The damage to her wrist remained for the rest of Nichola's life, so she hid it beneath a ribbon of black silk. As her life unfolded, Nichola realised that everything that John predicted had come true, so naturally, she dreaded the onset of her 47th birthday. However, that day came and passed, and Nichola found herself still alive. For the next year, she worried and fretted that every day would be her last until her 48th birthday loomed and she basked in relief. On the morning of her 48th birthday, Nichola celebrated with a party. She invited her family and her friends, new and old, including a churchman she and her family had known, for very many years.

As the party progressed, Nichola announced her age. 'I did not think I would be here,' she said. 'I am now forty-eight.'

The churchman looked confused, and then slowly shook his head. 'No,' he said. 'You are only forty-seven.'

Shocked, Nichola tried to argue, but the churchman had

known her for years. 'I looked at the registry of your birth recently,' he told her. 'You are only forty-seven.' Perhaps the churchman expected Nichola to be pleased that she was a year younger, but instead, she was terrified. Running upstairs, she hurriedly wrote her last will and died before midnight.

That is a poignant little story that begs several questions. If John had not appeared before her when she was younger, would Nichola have died on her birthday? Was he placing a curse on her? Was Nichola's death the result of auto-suggestion? We will never know the answer; however, there is a disturbing possibility that the whole tale may be a re-enactment of a much older story, or possibly proof of an ancient Irish tradition.

You see, there is a very similar story from the ninth century, where two students and foster brothers were talking about death. One said that when their friends die, 'they never come back again with news of the land to which they go.' The two foster brothers then agreed they would be different; they agreed that whoever died first would return to the other within a month. One of the foster-brothers died shortly afterwards, with the other burying him and waiting for his return.

When the dead brother did not come, the survivor began to curse him, and shouted at the Holy Trinity, and, as the story said, 'his soul begged the Trinity to let it talk with him.' As the living brother was in his hut, he banged his head and fell dead. His soul rose, saw his own body and thought it was his foster brother. 'This is bad,' the soul said, 'to bring me a dead body.' The soul wandered around, still believing it was within its body and wondering why people did not reply to its conversation. Eventually, the soul returned to the church and saw its foster brother.

'You have been a long time coming; yours was a bad promise.'

'I have come many a time,' the foster brother said, 'and would be beside your pillow, pleading with you and you did not hear; for the dense body does not hear the light ethereal tenuous soul.'

The foster brother told the wandering soul to return to its body, saying he would be alive for a year. The restless soul obeyed, and the corpse came back to life for another year, after which it died, and the soul ascended to heaven.

The tales are not quite the same, but share a similar theme of a promise between foster siblings, a return from the dead and a prophesy, yet they are hundreds of years apart, as we measure time in this life. Is one the more modern retelling of the other? Or are both stories only a dim realisation of life beyond death and the ties that bind us through promises and human relationships?

We will only find out the truth after death releases us from the torments of mortality.

TWENTY

MORE GHOSTS

MURDERS, massacres and executions punctuate Irish history.
During the various occupations of Ireland by England and
later Great Britain, justice could be patchy at best and non-
existent at worst. The trial of Myles Joyce and the Maamtrasna Murders in County Galway was a case in point. Joyce,
or to give him his real, Gaelic, name, Maolra Seoighe, was a
Gaelic speaker who did not understand a word of the court
case, which was held in English, with a defending solicitor
who did not speak a word of Gaelic.

The murder was real enough, with five members of a
local family butchered in Maamtrasna, county Galway in
August 1882, during the Irish Land Wars. The murderer, or
murderers, shot two men of the Joyce family and bludgeoned
three women to death. Eight men, including Myles Joyce,
were arrested and found guilty on the evidence of a paid
informer. Earl Spencer, the Lord Lieutenant of Ireland, paid
the informers while George Bolton, the Crown prosecutor,
allegedly withheld evidence. One of the informers who iden-
tified the supposed murderers was nowhere near the scene

of the crime and therefore in no position to point out anybody. That seemed unimportant to the Prosecution. At that time, Ireland was simmering with unrest, an assassin had recently murdered the Chief Secretary in Phoenix Park in Dublin, and across the Irish Sea, the British public wanted proof that the Rule of Law applied to Ireland as well as to Britain. In other words, they wanted an execution or two.

The judge condemned Joyce and another two men to death. William Marwood, the British government's official executioner, hanged the three men on the 15th December, 1882 in Galway Jail, despite a desperate plea by Joyce's pregnant wife and Joyce's repeated claims of innocence. It is perhaps not surprising that the ghost of innocent Myles Joyce should return the very next month.

According to the story, or one of them, two soldiers were on guard duty at the jail when what they called a 'tall mystic figure' glided towards them and took hold of their rifles. According to the Kerry Independent, the matron and warders of the jail applied for transfers soon after. A slightly different version of the story says that a soldier of the Connaught Rangers, the Devil's Own 88th Foot was on duty outside Galway Jail but went AWOL (Absent Without Leave.) At his court-martial in the newly built Renmore Barracks, the soldier's defence was that the ghost of Myles Joyce had appeared to him and frightened him into running away. Unfortunately, the officers of the court disbelieved him, and he spent the next two months in a military jail. In 2018, the Irish government gave Myles Joyce a posthumous pardon, hopefully giving his soul some peace and settling down his ghost.

Some Irish ghosts are well known. Others appeared once or twice and have been forgotten, except by the people who had the supernatural experience. One such incident happened in 1922 in Government House.

Hartley Patterson was one of two policemen on duty while the house was being readied for the Duke of Abercorn, the first governor. Patterson saw a police sergeant appear a few yards away, ignore him entirely and walk through a door. Patterson followed to find the door locked and bolted. No human being could have gone through without unbolting and unlocking the door.

The next night, shortly after midnight, Patterson and a colleague heard heavy footsteps in the house. They followed the sounds through a series of three rooms without seeing anything.

His colleague was unconcerned at having a ghost sharing the house and after a while, they 'looked forward to its company' as Patterson said. 'And we could always tell what time it was by its passing.' That ghost disappeared into history.

Sometimes ghosts are not all they appear to be. For instance, in December 1934, the town of Bangor was on high alert for a strange apparition that walked Princetown Road. Half the residents of the street heard mysterious footsteps on the road, yet when they looked out of the window, they saw nothing. After half an hour of fearful uncertainty, they saw something white on the road. The rumour spread that it was a ghost. More people gathered to watch this ghost until it came closer to them. Only then did they see that it was a swan, not just any swan but one named Gandhi, which was well known to many of the people in Bangor. The point of this story is that so many people believed there was a ghost in the first place.

The next story in this chapter is a little longer and comes from the seventeenth- century. It seems that at Michaelmas

1662, the 25-year-old Francis Taverner, a strong, hardy man who was scared by neither man nor devil, was riding his horse not far from Belfast. Taverner was a servant-at-large to Lord Chichester, the Earl of Donegal and that night near Drum Bridge his horse stopped and refused to go any further. Dismounting, Taverner tried to persuade the horse to move, but despite all his efforts, the horse remained static, except for the shivering that Tavernier thought was due to fear.

As Taverner mounted again, determined to use his spurs and whip, he saw two horsemen riding toward him. They passed him without a word and, even more surprisingly without a sound. Their hooves seemed to glide over the road rather than clopping on the surface. Staring in amazement, Taverner was shocked when a third horseman appeared out of nowhere. While the first two riders had been unknown to Taverner, this third man wore a long white coat and had once been a friend.

'In the name of God,' Taverner said. 'Who are you?'

'I am James Haddock,' the man in white replied.

Taverner could say nothing, for Haddock had lived in the village of Malone but had died five years previously.

'You doubt me,' Haddock said. 'You may call to mind by this token. About five years ago, I and two other friends were at your father's house and you, your father's appointment, brought us some nuts; and therefore be not afraid.'

Taverner could remember the night. He asked Haddock, 'why do you appear to me and no other?'

'Because you are a man of more resolution than others,' Haddock said. 'If you will ride with me, I will acquaint you with a business.'

'I will not go with you,' Taverner had no intention of sharing the road with a trio of spirits, or whatever the apparitions were. 'I will go my own way.' Pushing forward his horse, which now seemed eager to move, Taverner rode homeward, battling through a sudden storm. Bowing his head before the blast, he was sure he heard loud noises, like somebody or something screaming and shouting, but such was the darkness of the night that he could scarcely see his hand in front of his face, let alone what was beyond the fringes of the road.

As the storm abated, the noises simultaneously ceased, and Taverner heard the crow of a cock, which he took to signify the dawning. Nearly falling from the back of his horse, Taverner sunk to his knees to pray, begging God for help to get him safely home.

That same night, James Haddock again appeared to Taverner, with a strange message. The 'likeness of Haddock' asked Taverner to visit the former Mrs Haddock, now the wife of a man named Davis, still living at Malone and using her maiden name of Elenor Welsh. Haddock and Welsh had a son together, who had been Haddock's heir, but Davis had taken over the property. Haddock now asked Taverner to approach Elenor Welsh and tell her that their son should again have the rights to the property.

Having delivered his message, Haddock disappeared. Naturally disturbed, Taverner did not approach Elenor Welsh with the news, thinking he would be mocked, thought of as mad or possibly treated as a witch. Perhaps Taverner's decision was not the wisest, for Haddock appeared the following night as he sat beside his wife at the fire. Haddock also appeared to Taverner the next night, and every night for a month, with the spirit looking more hideous each time. Taverner began to dread the nights and began to tremble at every appearance.

Although Taverner's wife was often present when Haddock appeared, she did not see the spirit. Instead, she saw her husband shaking while his face paled, making her believe he was seriously ill. Ultimately, Taverner could take no more. He travelled over to Malone and asked Elenor if her maiden name was Welsh. Elenor said it was, adding that there was another Elenor Welsh besides her. That stumped Taverner, who returned home without delivering his message. That night, Haddock did not appear as Taverner sat beside the fire, but when he lay in bed, the spirit appeared in his white coat.

'Have you delivered my message?' Haddock asked.

'I've been to see Elenor Welsh,' Taverner hedged.

The spirit looked more pleased than it had before, told Taverner not to be afraid and disappeared in a bright flash.

Hoping that the matter was ended, Taverner went back to sleep. For the next few days, there was no sign of Haddock and Taverner began to relax, until the spirit appeared again. In a variety of horrible forms, it threatened to tear Taverner to pieces unless he delivered the message. By now Taverner was terrified and travelled to Belfast to tell people about his experiences. As Taverner stayed with a shoemaker named Pierce, and a couple of servants of Lord Chichester, Haddock visited him once more. Pierce and the others saw Taverner's face alter and he began to shake.

When Haddock appeared opposite him, Taverner lifted a candle and asked it, 'in the name of God, why do you haunt me?'

'I haunt you because you have not delivered my message,' the spirit said and once again threatened to tear him to pieces, before quickly vanishing. By now seriously upset, Taverner rode to Lord Chichester's house and told His Lordship and the family chaplain all that had happened. The Chaplain, James South, advised Taverner to obey the spirit and deliver the message, promising to accompany him. South took Taverner to Dr Lewis Downes, the minister of Belfast, who at first did not believe the story at all, thinking it was some mental delusion. After being persuaded that the story was true. Dr Downes wondered if Taverner should indeed, deliver the message, as he thought that the spirit might be from the devil rather than the ghost of James Haddock. On consideration, Downes accompanied Taverner and South to Davis's house to see Elenor Welsh.

When Taverner eventually delivered his message, he at once found peace of·mind as the spirit no longer threatened him. Leaving the matter in the hands of Welsh, Taverner rode to his brother's house at Drumbridge and tried to put the whole terrifying affair behind him. After two nights, Haddock re-appeared.

'Leave me,' Taverner pleaded. 'I delivered your message.' He also asked if Davis would 'do me any hurt.' The spirit replied that he would threaten Davis if he 'attempted anything to your injury.' That meeting seems to be the last that Taverner saw of Haddock although, according to legend and story, the affair of Davis and his step-son reached the courts. It seems that Bishop Jeremy Taylor investigated the case and decided that the spirit was genuine. At a court in Carrickfergus, the jury decided in favour of young Haddock, son of the ghost, while Davis, who had tried to cheat him out of his possessions, later fell from his horse and broke his neck.

My next story is the last in this chapter and is cobbled together from several sources, including contemporary newspaper reports and the words of local people.

In the summer of 1846 a house in West Street, Drogheda was said to be haunted. The owner was a woollen-draper who did not wish to give his name when the story was told in the mayor's court later that year. I was unreliably informed that he might have been a Mr James Cairn, so that is the name I shall use.

The trouble started in early June when the night-time peace was disturbed by the rattling of chains and a succession of screams that alarmed the servant girls and had Mr Cairn out of bed and searching for a pistol or at least a stout walking stick. However, such tools are of no use at all against the residents of the Other Place, and Mr Cairn's counter-attack proved fruitless. The noises began at midnight, prompt, and lasted for about an hour before subsiding.

Tiring of the nocturnal adventures, Mr Cairn called a family gathering to discuss what they could do to alleviate the problem. The members of the household, wife, servants and apprentices, all agreed that the house must be haunted. As soon as Mr Cairns informed the neighbours why he was lurking around with a candle in the wee small hours, they also thought there must be a ghost.

Now that he knew what caused the upsets, Mr Cairns set about protecting his house in every way he could. After praying for divine protection, he obtained a plentiful supply of Holy Water from the local priest and sprinkled it around every room and on the stairs and landings. Asking his servants and apprentices not to insult the spirit in case it became angry, Mr Cairns knew he had done all he could. Satisfied that nothing evil could penetrate his defences, Mr Cairns bid his household a good night and retired to bed.

The ghost returned. Night after night, from midnight to one in the morning, the house reverberated to the sounds of clanking chains and horrible screams. The servant girls became nervous wrecks, seeing ghosts wherever they looked, even in daylight, when the shadow of a passing carriage would metamorphose into a terrible demon and the spirit would appear before them in every room and once even on the ceiling of their shared bedroom, where it danced a fandango, upside down on the ceiling. One positive effect was a sudden upsurge in religion as the girls became regular church attendees, to the delight of the parish priest. Mrs Cairns was more upset when Mary, one of her maids fainted dead away at the supposed sight of the ghost.

As the second servant looked likely to join her friend on the floor, Mrs Cairns tried to help Mary by burning feathers under her nose. Mary remained static until Mr Cairns forced a mouthful of brandy between her lips, at which point one of the apprentice lads suggested that he felt faint as well.

'I saw it,' Mary whispered. 'I saw a ghost!'

'What did you see, Mary?' Mrs Cairns asked. 'Tell us what you saw.'

'It was a spirit,' Mary said. 'It was dressed in a long white robe, with deep-set eyes in a very pale face and from its mouth came a sulphurous flame, brighter than a hundred candles. Its bones rattled when it walked.'

'No wonder you fainted,' said kind-hearted Mrs Cairns.

That experience was more than sufficient for Mary, for the very next night her nerve broke. Screaming in terror, she fled the house and ran to that of Mr Duggan in the same street. 'Mr Cairns' house,' she declared, 'is haunted by a legion of devils, and I won't return for untold thousands.'

Standing at his front door, Mr Duggan surveyed the sobbing girl with her bare feet and her night-dress in disarray. 'Something has to be done,' he decided, as he ushered inside to the care of his wife.

Mr Cairns tried everything he could, but the ghost refused to leave his house. It screamed, knocked things down, moved shoes, hats and fire-irons, rattled the maidservants' door and generally terrorised the place until Mr Cairns declared defeat and sent the females of his household to a quieter place deep in the country. He remained behind with his male apprentices, for the house was his place of business as well as his home. In his mind, he knew what was happening. The ghost was one of his long-dead ancestors who were, as he said himself, 'in a bad state in the Other World.' There was nothing for it but to get professional help, so Mr Cairns called in the priest to exorcise the unwanted guest.

The priest arrived with bell, book, candle and all good wishes. He said masses in the house and ordered the spirit to depart. That same night the noises were worse than ever, with the spirit mocking the priest and all his wiles.

'It must be a Protestant ghost,' Mr Cairns said, 'or a heathen, not to be affected by the words of God.'

Protestant, heathen or just plain nasty, the spirit increased its antics, even throwing stones at Mr Cairns as he lay in bed. Eventually, Mr Cairns could stand it no longer and left the house at night for the sanctuary of a hotel. Now only three beings lived in the house: two apprentices and the spirit.

With Cairns away, there was a period of calm. The apprentices reported that the noises had ended and Mr Cairns returned home, albeit a trifle nervously. When nothing happened for a few days, he sent for his wife and the maids, who also came in, trembling.

'It's safe,' Mr Cairns assured them.

The household settled down, and things seemed normal for a while. Mrs Cairns and the maids began to relax, no longer jumping at every creak of the floorboards and rumble of wind in the chimney. And then the noises started again. Until then, the older and larger of the apprentices had been mostly unaffected by the disturbances, but that night the spirit seemed to concentrate on him. At first the youth ignored the sounds, then he hid under the bedclothes and finally, finding that a few layers of cloth were no defence against the malicious spirit, he leapt out of bed, tripped over his blankets and tumbled head over heels down the stairs in a tangle of bare legs, flailing arms and flapping nightshirt. According to one account, he was shouting, 'oh Holy Mother, Mercy! Mercy! I'll repent.' Although what his sins had been, nobody was sure.

The noise he made naturally woke up the rest of the household, who scrambled out of bed in time to see this six-foot tall, gangly youth dressed in his white nightgown at the foot of the stairs. Believing that the spirit had assumed a concrete form, the Cairn family, man, women and servants, burst open the door and ran screaming into the street.

'Holy Matthew, Mark, Luke and John,' they shouted as they fled from their house. Not until they passed through West Street and up Lawrence's Street did the supposed ghost let them know he was only an apprentice.

'It's me,' he said. 'I am murdered! Oh, my poor ribs!'

None of them returned home that night. Of the entire household, there remained one lad who was not afraid of the ghost. This remaining apprentice, Elisha John Rorke only laughed at its antics and refused to be cowed.

'You're a brave man,' Mr Cairns said.

'Not at all,' the apprentice shook his head. 'This ghost must be a Protestant, and as I am of that persuasion, it leaves me alone. I think you should try another priest, Mr Cairns.'

Summoning all his courage, Cairns returned to his house, bringing his terrified family with him. After that, things only got worse, with the spirit picking on Cairns, bombarding him with stones and bottles. The priest's efforts were all for nothing as the vision continued to dominate the house, ignoring blessings, curses, bell, book, candle, holy water and the pleas of the Cairns family.

As well as the priest, other people tried to shift the stubborn spirit, including an optimistic man named James

Treeves. By that time the Cairns family were weary of enthusiastic amateurs, so watched without emotion as Treeves arrived, armed with a large bottle of Holy Water and a dedicated desire to cleanse the property of its unwanted visitor. Rather than do his stuff during the day and then going home, Treeves asked for a door-key and left. He returned in secrecy that night and waited in the dark of a passage, wishing to see this ghost for himself. Eventually, around midnight, he saw the spirit slithering along a passage. As it neared Cairns' bedroom, the ghost began to rattle chains and moan.

Approaching with his bottle of water poised, Treeves was astonished to find the apprentice Rorke instead of a spirit, and Rorke was rattling chains and holding a capful of stones, all ready to launch at poor Mr Cairns.

'What's to do?' Treeves shouted. 'You're no ghost!'

At Treeves' words, doors banged open, and the anxious faces of the family peered out, with Cairns holding a walking stick in trembling hands and the servant girls clinging to each other in a mixture of terror and tiredness. They all saw Treeves holding the apprentice by the scruff of his neck.

While the household was surprised, kindly Mrs Cairns was furious that Rorke had frightened her servants and took instant revenge on Rorke with the business end of a broom. The servants watched, encouraging Mrs Cairns when she flagged.

'Go on, Mrs Cairns, give it to him hot!' The older servant girl approved.

Only when Mrs Cairns tired was Rorke deposited for his safety in the watchhouse. The watchman questioned him sternly, threatening to hand him back to Mrs Cairns' broomstick if he did not tell the truth.

'I'm truly dead,' the apprentice said. 'Could you drag the River Boyne for my corpse, for the fish are eating me?'

'You're no more dead than I am,' the watchman said. 'You're as much a ghost as a tankard of porter, and here's Mrs Cairns back for you, with her broom.'

Cringing at the thought, the apprentice admitting he was very much alive and had done it as a joke. And that ended both the story of the ghost of Drogheda's West Street and this chapter of ghosts. The next chapter delves back to the Dark Ages to find out how so many Irish people can come from such a small island.

TWENTY-ONE
THE IRISH DIASPORA

IRELAND MAY BE a small island on the western fringe of
Europe, but the Irish seem to have populated half the world.
Indeed, the Irish have a habit of obeying the Biblical exhorta-
tion to go forth and multiply, or sometimes to multiply and go
forth. Perhaps the reason was the desperate poverty and occasional famines that struck the island of Ireland, or maybe it is
due to the fantastic fecundity of the people.

Take, for instance, Niall of the Nine Hostages. He was a
fourth-century Irish king who enlivened the sea between
Ireland and Britain with raids. That is one aspect of history
that people often forget , fleets of curraghs from Ireland
crossed the sea to Britain to grab booty and slaves. One of
these slaves was shocked at the pagan nature of Ireland and
returned to spread Christianity. His name was Patrick, a
name which is often taken to represent all things Irish now.
He may have come from the British kingdom of Strathclyde,
in present-day Scotland, or from what is now Wales, but he
was undoubtedly a Celtic Briton.

It is unlikely that Niall kidnapped Patrick in person, but

the possibility is intriguing if nothing else. Niall himself had a strange background. His father, Eochaid, was High King of Ireland, who was married to Mong Find, a beautiful brunette who bore him four strapping sons, Fergus, Aillil, Fiachra and Brian. Note the absence of Niall in that distinguished list. Despite his evident physical attraction to his wife, Eochaid fell in love with another woman. At that time the Irish were noted raiders, and one of Eochaid's hostages was Caireann, a Saxon woman, presumably a very early settler in what is now known as England, or possibly a slave of the Romans. As much as Eochaid loved Caireann, Mong Find despised her with all the venom that a spurned Irish wife could have – and that is a lot of venom.

As the wife and queen, Mong Find was in charge of the king's possessions, including the lovely Caireann. The queen seems to have been a bit of a tartar, or perhaps she became bitter when her husband became overly affectionate with his Saxon slave. Either way, Mong Find made Caireann's life hell, although nobody had invented that term yet. Among the tasks Mong Find made Ciaireann perform was to carry the water from the well, or the spring, to the house. Although some people wished to help Ciareann, they were too scared of Mong Find to act.

When Eochaid got Ciareann pregnant, Mond Find worked the Saxon even harder, hoping to create a miscarriage. The plan did not work. One day Ciareann gave birth while still working at her daily drudge. Terrified of the queen, she left her newborn son on the ground and continued to work. The child lay there, unwanted and neglected until a man named Torna lifted him. Torna was a poet, and like many of his profession, he could tap into other powers. As soon as he saw the baby, Torna knew that he was destined to greatness. Torna knew that this child would grow up to be the

High King of Ireland. Lifting the baby, Torna carried him away, named him Niall and brought him up. Many years later, when Niall had grown to a man, Torna brought back Niall to Tara.

By some miracle, Ciareann had survived the years of unceasing labour, so when Niall somehow recognised his mother, he removed her from her torture, dressed her as befitted the mother of a king and placed her on a throne. Naturally, the queen protested, which did not concern Niall in the slightest. Now Mong Find was unhappy that Niall had survived and insisted that Eochaid should choose his heir, hoping that the king favoured one of her sons. Instead, Eochaid asked Sithchean, the royal druid, to find out which of his sons was best suited to be king. Druids were cunning men, possibly magicians, with the name allegedly coming from the word dru, an oak, as the druids were said to worship oak trees. There is even a poem written by St Columba, *is e mo drai Crist mac De*, 'Christ the Son of God is my Druid.' There was also a Druid motto that said 'Be brave, that you may survive among the blessed.'

As well as holy men, druids were renowned for their wisdom. There is a passage in the *Ancient Laws of Ireland* that says 'For such was the rule of Ulster. The men of Ulster must not speak before the King, and the King must not speak before his druids.'

With all this power in him, Sithchean devised a test for the sons. He ordered all five young men into the royal forge, with instructions to make a sword for himself. The instant they entered the forge, Sithchean shut the door and set the building on fire. The weapon making had only been a ploy; the druid would assess the character of the princes by what they rescued from the flames.

When Brian was first out, with the smith's hammers in

his hands, Sithchean predicted that he would be a strong fighting man. Fiachra rescued a barrel of beer, which Sithchean worked out as meaning that the prince was a man of science and art. Next was Aillil, who held a pile of weapons; the druid thought he would be a man ready to revenge any wrong done to the people of Ireland. When Fergus came second last, carrying a bundle of sticks, Sithchean was not impressed, saying he was probably impotent. Last out was Niall, holding the anvil, the symbol of the smithy.

'Ah,' said Sithchean. 'Here is your future king. Niall will be a solid anvil for the people of Ireland.'

Strangely, Mong Find was not pleased. She tried to arrange a quarrel among her sons, during which Niall would be quietly murdered by the other four. However, Torna stepped in before anybody was seriously hurt. There were other incidents between the five sons of Eochaid, such as the hunt where they killed a deer but had neglected to bring water with them. Now in Ireland, that should not have posed a problem, for there is a plethora of rivers and lochs, but for some reason, they were in an area strangely dry.

The brothers sent Fergus to find water. He found a well, with a wrinkled, dirty old hag standing guard. When Fergus asked if he could fetch water from the well, the old hag said he would have to kiss her first. Refusing her request, Fergus returned to his brothers and said he had not found anything. One by one, the other brothers searched for water, and each met the hag. Only Fiachra gave her a brief kiss. The hag smiled, telling him that two of his descendants would be kings. However, she did not allow him any water. Fiachra also reported he could not find water.

That left only Niall. When the hag asked for a kiss, rather than baulk, Niall offered not only a kiss but also to

make love to her. That was the first example of Niall's unde-
niable attraction to the opposite sex. The hag did not object
to the attention of this handsome and sensual young man, so
within a few moments, they were lying on the long grass
beside the well. As in all the best stories, the old hag transformed into a stunningly beautiful young woman. Naturally,
this woman also had the power to foretell the future. She said
that Niall was destined to become king, as were his
descendants.

'Take water from my well,' the young and now attractive
seer said. 'Let your brothers see it, but give them nothing
until they agree that you have dominion over them.'

By the time Niall returned to his half-brothers, they were
dying of thirst, which is a strange thing in Ireland. Niall
waited until they were in very desperate straits before he said
he would save them only if they agreed he should be king.
Faced with a horrible death by thirst, the four brothers could
only concur with Niall.

As High King of Ireland, ruling from Tara, Niall subdued
the island of Ireland and expanded his power across the sea to
the nations of Britain. Niall was too sensible to try and
conquer the lands on the eastern side of the Irish Sea; instead,
he took hostages from each country, so he had the nine
hostages that gave him his name. As long as he held these
hostages, he knew these eastern nations could not invade
Ireland. That little history poses as many questions as it
answers, such as when he reigned.

According to legend, Niall was king from 379 until 405.
He was also said to be a great lover. Was he? Well, if the story
of Niall has been strange so far, the legacy he left might be
even more curious. Professor Dan Bradley of Trinity College
did an extensive DNA analysis to discover that Niall has left
around three million descendants. Now, I don't pretend to

understand much of what follows; it is all taken from the work of other people. About a fifth of all Irishmen in the north-west of the island have the R1b1c7 Y-chromosome. That north-western area was where the O'Neills, the U Neill, or descendant of Neill, had their base. Is it possible that many, if not the majority, of these people, have a common descendant in Niall of the Nine Hostages?

Outside of Ireland, there are millions of people of Irish descent, with an estimated one in fifty European-descended people in New York alone reportedly descended from Niall. That is a tremendous figure in anybody's book. According to the computer, around eighty million people claim Irish descent, including thirty-six million North Americans. That is a large number from a small island, and somewhat strange when one considers the difficulties that have beset Ireland throughout the centuries. However, it is a hint that the Irish are rather special people, I think, which is a fact with which they would not disagree. Facts speak for themselves.

TWENTY-TWO
THE FOLKLORE OF IRELAND

As in any ancient country, Ireland has collected a vast store of folklore, folk medicine and general advice based on natural occurrences. To write them all would take at least an encyclopaedia so that this shortish chapter will mention only a few of the thousands of snippets of such wisdom.

I gleaned some of these pieces from newspapers and books, some from talking to people in pubs, shops and on quiet roads in various parts of Ireland. I am sure that the word spread that a strange Scotsman was wandering the byways asking stupid questions. I must say that rarely did I meet with a rude answer; the Irish people proved every bit as hospitable as their friendly reputation suggests.

Sometimes the simple sayings or fragments of folk wisdom relate to ancient superstition, such as the belief that saying the Lord's Prayer backwards can be used as a curse. On the other hand, people can use a horseshoe for Good. It was common for people to nail a horseshoe above the door of their stable to keep the horse safe from witches or fairies. That belief may be related to the idea that the fairies were afraid of cold iron, which furthers the belief that they came from a race that was in Ireland before the Iron Age. However certain plants such as hazel, broom or mountain ash, were equally repugnant to them.

Some of the folk beliefs refer to cures for common complaints. Toothache is still a demon even today. In old Ireland, people believed that chewing a yarrow leaf would cure the nagging pain. Another method of curing toothache was more complicated. The sufferer had to visit the local churchyard and kneel on a grave. Any grave seems to do; no particular one was specified. While on the grave, the sufferer had to say three paters and three aves for the soul of the inhabitant. With that task completed, the sufferer would next pull some grass from the now-blessed grave and chew on it, although he or she was not allowed to swallow.

Toothache must have been pretty prevalent in old Ireland, to judge by the many cures. If one carries the two jawbones of a haddock in one's pocket, toothache would never strike. Why is that? Well, religion comes into it again, for a haddock is marked with the thumb and finger of the Lord, as an examination will show. Naturally, old bones are better than new, for they are closer to the time when the miracle of God's handprint arrived.

Cures for other pains could also have a religious angle. For example, if a woman or man suffered from back-ache, he or she could hang a hare's foot around their neck. Hares were strongly connected to witchcraft as it was, but these hare's feet had an additional power if the wearer also attached a written charm:

May Peter take, may Paul take, may Michael take the pain away, the cruel pain that kills the back and the life and darkens the light of the eyes.

This strange combination of Christianity and paganism

lingered in many aspects of Irish folklore and life. The Irish were always known for their skill in horsemanship, with Irish horse whisperers still existing. A horse whisperer is a man or woman who can tame an unruly horse or train one up to various skills, simply by using his voice. The gift is hereditary, passed through the generations. Only the whisperer knows all the tricks of the trade, but legend says that one method they used was to whisper the Apostles' Creed into their ears. On a Friday, the whisperer would whisper the Creed into the horse's right ear, and on the following Wednesday into the left ear, with the whisperer repeating the procedure until the horse was docile.

In case you were unsure, the Apostles Creed is a statement of Christian belief that begins like this:

> I believe in God, the Father almighty,
> Creator of heaven and earth.
> I believe in Jesus Christ, God's only Son, our
>   Lord,
> Who was conceived by the Holy Spirit,

and continues to the final Amen.

In the mediaeval period and possibly for long before, the Irish people were afraid of the power of fairies. From the latter half of the sixteenth century, witches joined or replaced fairies as figures of fear, and nervous people used many of the same preventative defences. There were many ways to protect a house against the power of witchcraft. One was to use candles hallowed on Candlemas Day. Another was to plant a house-leek on the roof. Incidentally, the leek also gave protection from fire and lightning. Even more straightforward was to drink salt water: salt was thought to be holy and is still used by witches today. The Romans also valued salt very highly, so perhaps the use of salt predates Christianity by some time. Branches of the rowan tree were useful, or even a necklace made from the bright red rowan berries.

Fear of the fairies, the people of the Sidh lingered long after the onset of industrialisation of Europe. If any mysterious illness struck a man or woman, people wondered if he was 'elf-struck', suffering from a fairy spell. However, there was a cure: crush a dozen foxglove leaves in a cup and drink the solution. That might work, or it could kill the sufferer. The name foxglove comes from Folk's Glove, with the folk in question being the fairy-folk. Another, less drastic solution was to write a sentence from the gospels on a piece of paper and fasten it around the neck. The best was the first three verses of St John's Gospel. *'In the beginning, was the Word, and the Word was with God, and the Word was God.'* You might already know them, or have them unconsciously within your mind, for cock's crow them early every morning. All you have to do is listen and understand the language of these strutting birds. Why do they strut? They strut because they know the Word of God, of course. Religion or superstition imbued every action of old Ireland.

Fairies did have their uses, if approached with politeness and treated with caution. They could provide spells to cure sickness or to cause love between a man and a woman. Naturally, there were various stipulations; when somebody carried the love message or sickness cure from the fairy to her customer, the carrier could not speak or even look behind them until they handed over what they carried. For the potion to be most effective, the person for whom it was intended had to swallow it immediately without anybody else touching it. I would treat the Sidh with respect and avoid them if possible. Dealing with the unknown always carries an element of risk.

Witches were notorious for cursing the simple, essential things of life, such as cattle and butter, everyday units in an overwhelmingly rural environment. As always, there is a way of repelling witchcraft. If a housewife placed a red-hot horseshoe under the butter churn, witches could not make the cows go dry or put charms to steal the butter. This last was easy; all the witch had to do was say: 'all to me and none to thee' again and again until the curse took effect. A witch could also collect dew from the grass on the first of May, or remove a lighted coal, or any fire from the farmhouse on that day. It was thought to be inadvisable to give away water, salt or fire on the first of May. Once again there is the use of iron and salt, harking back to some forgotten memory of pagan religion and possibly to the advent of Iron Age peoples into an island that did not know that metal. The impact of superior technology always had a fearful effect on those who lacked that knowledge.

In old Ireland, witches and evil spirits were a daily fear. Today, with our fast-paced twenty-first-century lifestyles, our supposed sophistication and everyday technology, it is easy to scoff at the old beliefs. Now, think of an Irish winter in the seventeenth century, with no electric lights or any powered gadgets. There were no proper roads, no decent transport system, no trained doctors or nurses, no education for the mass of the population. People were at the mercy of the weather and their fears, the superstitions, suppositions and stories that had been part of life for hundreds of generations. While people remembered the tales of fairies and demons and saw the gaunt ruins of shattered castles and stretches of moorland where the blood of men had soaked into the ground, the long dark of winter surrounded them and the gloom of warfare approached from the east.

Try that for a month and see how quickly the veneer of

modern civilisation strips away to leave the stark reality. Stand alone amid the limestone desert of western Connaught, or within the dark shadow of the Sperrin Mountains, or under the dripping stark trees around Cobh, or the haunting grimness of the Burren and listen to the darkness. Then tell me that you don't believe in witches or fairies.

If you find that you do believe, maybe only a little bit, then you better take some precautions. One of the simplest methods is to carry a sprig of yarrow or St John's Wort. It seems to be the little pellucid spots which grace the leaves of St John's Wort which scare the devil, for his evil darts caused them in the first place. The best way of using yarrow before going on a journey is as follows: pluck ten leaves from a yarrow plant and immediately discard one. That will be a bribe to the evil spirits so they will leave you alone. Place the other nine in your right shoe, under the heel. After that, the devil cannot hurt you. I don't think even yarrow works against modern motor vehicles driven by idiots though, which are probably every bit as dangerous as an evil spell.

Plants and other natural things were central to life, with every variety of tree and plant having its own story and use. As well as yarrow leaves, any walker could find a stout stick to help ease away the miles. Hazel or blackthorn is possibly the best or mountain ash if you are nervous about fairies. One staff to avoid is hawthorn, for as you already know, the fairies hold the hawthorn as sacred. They do not approve of humans using their tree, let alone cutting the wood and humans must never bring hawthorn blossom into the house. The flowers will attract the fairies, and once they are in the house, they will never leave and cause you all sorts of grief.

To continue on that subject, if you have a front and back door, don't have both open at the same time on the night before Mayday or the last day of October, in case the fairies decide to make a road through the house. If the fairies start marching through, they might easily steal the children or the butter. I am not sure what the attraction of butter was for fairies and witches, but they certainly liked it. They also like a saucer of milk or fragments of cake, so if you wish to keep on their right side, leave such delicacies out at night. If the fairies don't find it, a hedgehog might so that can only be good. A final note about butter: if an Irish lad fancied a girl, but was too shy to approach her, he could win her heart with butter. All he had to do was find some freshly churned butter and place it carefully on a brand-new plate. Then he had to find a spot where a water mill stood beside a tree, invite her there and hand over the butter while whispering a charm that a wise woman or a fairy had told him. Unfortunately, I never could find out what the charm was, so to learn it; you will have to find a friendly fairy. Try the cake-and–milk bribe for that but proceed with caution for the people of the Sidh are tricky creatures and can easily entice you.

I'll close this small chapter with a few unconnected bits and pieces. First of all, I'll put in a word about egg shells. These are useful things, and not only because they stop the inside of the egg from falling out. In old Ireland, if a chicken hatched from an egg, the shells were retained and hung up in the belief that they repelled predatory hawks from swooping down to grab the young chicks. There were other superstitions regarding eggs as well: grooms were utterly forbidden from eating eggs, while even the owner of a horse had to be careful. He or she had to eat an even number of eggs and to wash their hands, or bad fortune would befall the horse. I'm not sure of the connection between horses and eggs, although I suspect that there is a fear of witchcraft there, somewhere.

Lastly, I will add a nasty little curse. If you happened to admire a person of the opposite sex, only to find that she or he was already attached to somebody else, the solution was simple. All you had to do was find a new grave, scoop up a handful of soil from the top and shake it between the lovers. They would be quarrelling within the hour and soon would split up, leaving the field open for you. On that gruesome little note, I will close this chapter and open one that includes Ireland's favourite saint and a major sinner.

TWENTY-THREE

THE DEVIL, A DEMON AND A SAINT

Most countries have legends about the devil, or the equivalent of a devil, the personification of a force of evil. Ireland is no exception, given that religion has been a major driving force of the island for many centuries.

Loftus Hall is a large house that rears prominently from the land near the coast on the Hook Peninsula in County Wexford, exposed to all the force of the maritime climate. In case you had not realised, Ireland is known as the Emerald Isle because the rain keeps her grass green. The rain can come in soft gentleness, or it can be driven in face-scouring fury, with a wild wind blasting Ireland as if determined to blow this stubborn island off the map. It was on one of the latter occasions when a ship anchored off the Hook Peninsula on County Wexford. A tall, handsome, dark-haired man disembarked and stalked up to Lotus Hall with his long cloak brushing the ground and a fancy scarlet cravat protecting his throat.

The tall man knocked at the door of the hall and asked for shelter for the night. Only too pleased to have some new company, Lord Tottenham brought him in and offered him warmth, rest and refreshment. The man fitted in immediately with his charming smile and debonair manners. Indeed, Lord Tottenham's youngest daughter Anne was incredibly smitten with the stranger. Lord and Lady Tottenham exchanged glances, smiled and allowed the friendship to develop as there were few eligible young men in that part of Ireland and with them present to chaperone their daughter, nothing could go far wrong. When the evening came, the Tottenhams had the servants draw the curtains and build up the fire. Lord Tottenham had the card tables brought out, and the entire company sat around the green baize while the faces and numbers flicked from deck to table.

Anne was slightly nervous being in the company of a man with whom she believed she was falling in love, so it is not surprising that when she was dealing, she fumbled and dropped one of the cards. Stooping to pick it up, she saw that the stranger wore no shoes under his cloak. What was worse; rather than feet, he had the cloven hooves of a goat.

Letting out a terrified scream when she realised her handsome new sweetheart was none other than Satan himself, Anne rushed from the room, shouting: 'He's the devil!' As soon as Anne said the words, the devil did not hang around in Loftus Hall. Rising from his chair, he turned into a raging ball of fire and shot through the ceiling, up through the roof and away. Anne screamed again; she was never the same woman after meeting the devil. Although the devil had gone, he left a souvenir of his visit in the shape of the hole he burned in the roof. That hole still exists as proof that the devil visited. If you choose to visit, select a dark night when the wind is howling, for the best effect.

Now, from one extreme to the other, this chapter will

move from the epitome of evil to the symbol of eternal good with a weird story.

When St Patrick returned to Ireland to spread Christianity, he also banished the snakes. Some think that the term snakes was a euphemism for the druids, but it is a fact that there are no poisonous snakes in the island of Ireland, while there are in the neighbouring island of Britain. At the same time as he fought the snakes, Patrick met a demon called Caorthannach, who was said to be Satan's mother.

Naturally, the two fought and thankfully St Patrick won. His method appears simple:

Patrick climbed the hill, now known as Croagh Patrick in Mayo on Ireland's wild west coast, and gathered all the snakes and demons around him. An eleventh-century author wrote of this time '*When Patrick, glorious in grace, was suffering on goodly Cruach – an anxious, toilsome time for him... God sent to comfort him a flock of spotless angelic birds.*'

With or without the birds, Patrick had to combat the thousands of snakes and crawling creatures. Once the serpents gathered around him, Patrick ordered them out of Ireland. At first, the snakes and demons refused to go; they were quite happy terrorising the good people of Ireland, thank you very much. But Patrick was not to be defeated by the forces of evil. He just happened to have a consecrated bell with him, which was probably standard kit for a saint in the bad old days, and anyway, an angel had given it to him as he endured a forty-day fast. Lifting the bell, Patrick rang it to reinforce his order.

That did the trick. At the sound of the holy clatter, the snakes slithered down the mountain, across the country, into the sea and drowned. However, the demons, being devilishly clever, were not so keen to destroy themselves. They ran away, only to hide in a place now called the Demon's Hollow. They remained there, watching through viciously hard eyes. St Patrick followed, lifted his bell again and threw it among them. The sound of the angel's bell forced the demons away, and this time, they did not stop until they reached the sea, where they drowned.

Or rather, most of them did. One extremely unpleasant demon still avoided Patrick's command and wriggled away. This demon was Caorthannach, known as the fire-spitter. Patrick was not a saint for nothing: he saw Caorthannach escape and called for a fast horse. Even then, Ireland was known for its quality horses, so when a man brought the fastest horse in the land to him, Patrick mounted swiftly and chased after the demon-snake.

Round and round Ireland they sped, with Caorthannach using her fiery breath to dry up every lough and river and poison every well so that Patrick would be too thirsty to continue. Rather than drink, Patrick prayed for help. God must have answered his prayers, for Patrick overtook the demon-snake to arrive at Hawk's Rock in County Sligo before Caorthannach. Hawk's Rock is a very English-sounding name for a lump of stone in western Ireland. Perhaps I should use its much more evocative and probably older alternative name, *Carrick-na-shee-og*, which translates as the Rock of the Young Fairies. Patrick would have no difficulty locating this rock, which sits prominently on a hill near Coolaney. One version of the story says that Patrick's horse slipped here. He landed heavily, prayed for water and a spring appeared among the rocks, from which Patrick drank. Hiding behind the fairy's rock, he waited until Caorthannach approached, leapt out and said the holy word that banished the demon-snake to the ocean. Caorthannach drowned, but not before she left an ugly swell. By some miracle, this swell forced fresh water into the well that Patrick had created, some miles away. Even today, many centuries later, the water level in the well still rises and falls in an extraordinary fashiony.

The well, known as the Hawk's Well also has a pair of magic trout that only the faithful or the pure of heart can see. I did try, but alas, no trout appeared for me. I am not sufficiently pure. These trout have been in the well as long as the memory of Man, or Woman, who probably has a longer memory anyway. On the odd occasion, some unworthy persons have been said to take them away, but they always return. Others say that there is only a single trout. One day a man tried to bake that unfortunate fish, only for the trout to leap from the gridiron when it was half done and return to the well. Those who can see it claim that one side of it is marked with the pattern of the grid.

'Ah' I can sense you asking. 'What may this Hawk's Well be?'

Hawk's Well is one of the lesser known strange places of Ireland, and for that reason, it is all the more worthy of a visit. When I was there, I had a moment of glorious sunshine, followed by a grey blanket of Atlantic drizzle that seemed much more in keeping with its reputation for ancient demon-banishing. As with the rock, the well also has another name: Tubber Tullanaghan or Tullaghan Hill Holy Well. Despite the story, this well was here before St Patrick, as there were pagan rituals here that lasted until the nineteenth century. It was the Dublin-based Cardinal Cullen who forbade such rituals. Perhaps they still take place in secret: Ireland can be like that.

When I visited, there was a bit of a path to the Hawk's Well, not easy to follow despite the winter lack of vegetation. The water is murky, to put it mildly, which perhaps helps hide the two trout. On a clear day, the view must be immense, but my visit had only a few moments of clarity between long spells of grey drizzle. Better luck next time. There is a cairn nearby and a drystone wall, while the whole edifice is within an ancient fort. Perhaps this well provided drinking water for the inhabitants, thousands of years ago.

There is another legend here, one which predates Patrick and is anything but Christian. Briefly put, the story relates that a hero named Eremon decapitated his servant Gamh and tossed the head into the well, which is said to explain its slightly bitter taste. Other legends say that no fire can ever boil the well-water.

This place has been sacred for many centuries, reputedly to the Celtic goddess Aine. William Butler Yeats, the Irish poet and playwright, created a play about this well, with a story that from time to time it could make people immortal. In Yeats play, Cu Chulainn arrived to try the water but was persuaded by an old man not to try.

I cannot argue with Yeats. I can only say that St Patrick did an excellent job in banishing the snakes from Ireland, but the devil may still call from time to time. If you are unsure, look at the feet of any stranger to see if they are cloven.

TWENTY-FOUR
A CAUSEWAY FOR A GIANT

IT WOULD BE impossible to talk about strange Ireland without mentioning the coolest giant that island ever produced. His name was Finn Mac Cool, and he was possibly the most famous giant that Ireland ever produced. The correct spelling is Fionn mac Cumhaill, and people in Scotland also know his story well, although in the northern kingdom they call him Fingal.

You are bound to have heard of the Giant's Causeway. If you are fortunate, you might have visited that spectacular rock formation in County Antrim. If you are incredibly blessed, you may have seen these basaltic columns in good weather. I was not so lucky: I was drenched. It was still worth the visit, especially when my local guide told me some of the stories. It seems that Finn made his home on the north coast of Antrim, where he lived with Oonagh, his wife. Now they were a very contented pair of giants, except for one thing: Finn had a rival, a giant named Benandonner who lived in what is now Argyll in western Scotland. After a while, Finn grew tired of merely shouting insults across the water to Benandonner and challenged him to a fight.

'Come on then,' Benandonner said. 'Come on over, and we'll see if you are giant enough to take me on.'

Well, Finn was a bit reluctant to swim or even wade across as he did not like getting wet, so he thought he would build a bridge, or rather a causeway from Ireland to Scotland. Like so many people in old Ireland, Finn seems to have been an expert stonemason and formed a beautiful causeway from Antrim to Argyll. However, he had no sooner arrived in Scotland than he saw Benandonner for the first time. Although Finn was huge, the Scottish giant was massive, taller and bigger in every possible way.

'I'm not fighting a giant that size,' Finn said, and promptly retreated back to Ireland where Oonagh was waiting for him.

'You're in a hurry,' Oonagh said. 'Did you settle your argument with Benandonner?'

'I did not,' Finn said. 'He is much too big for me.' Finn looked over his shoulder. 'He's following me now, Oonagh. I need your help to hide.'

Well, it is difficult for a giant to hide as they are naturally quite large. Oonagh looked around for a haven. 'Leave it to me,' Oonagh said. 'We'll hide you in plain sight.'

'What does that mean?' Finn asked.

'You can be my baby,' Oonagh said. Making him an enormous cradle, she laid him inside, covered him in swaddling clothes and was singing a lullaby when Benandonner tramped over for the fight.

'Where is Finn?' Benandonner roared.

'Shush!' Oonagh reprimanded him severely. 'Can't you see that the baby is asleep?'

Benandonner shivered at the sight of the supposed baby.

'If that is Finn's child,' he said, 'Finn must be huge indeed, far too large for me to handle.' Rather than stay to fight, he turned around and ran back to Scotland. As he retreated, he destroyed the causeway behind him to ensure Finn did not follow, and that is the story of the Giant's Causeway. Naturally, the geologists will tell another story, but what do they know?

While we are on the theme of large things, I will mention another of Ireland's old timers. Scotland's Loch Ness Monster is arguably the most famous mythological creature in the world. If the Yeti or Bigfoot wish to argue, they are welcome to knock at my door to give their point of view. I promise that I will listen, albeit from behind the couch or some other safe place. However, Ireland also has its own rather unpleasant mythological creature.

The Dobhar Chu infests Glendale Lough in Leitrim. The name means water hound, while the monster is around seven feet long and is a cross between an otter and a dog. Unlike some creatures, the Dobhar Chu can hunt on land as well as in the water and humans are its prey. If you happen to be walking beside Glendale Lake in County Leitrim and hear a terrifying scream, don't bother to run: it will probably already be too late. The Dobhar Chu will get you.

How real is this creature? If you happen to visit Conwall Cemetery in Glendale, you might find a nearly-three-centuries old gravestone that carries a blurred image of a Dobhar Chu. According to legend, in September 1722, a woman named Grainne Ni Conalai was at the side of Glendale Lough, washing clothes. The Dobhar Chu came out of the lake, killed her and was perched on her body when her husband came from the house to see what was causing all the noise. The husband killed the monster and then killed a second that emerged from the lake, but that did not bring back his wife.

And that is about all that is known about that particular Dobhar Chu. Nobody seems to understand why the creature was there or what happened to it afterwards. Some say there never was a Dobhar Chu and the husband was merely covering up his murder of Grainne Ni Conalai, but I think that is mean. Of course, there is a monster; it is a bit shy, that's all.

There once was another monster on Scattery Island at the mouth of the River Shannon. Now uninhabited, the island of Scattery is also known as Inis Cathaigh, the island of Cathaig, a terrible monster that lived here. Fortunately, there was a saint on hand to end the menace. The Archangel Michael guided St Senan to a hill, from where Senan could see Cathaig. What he was would be enough to terrify any mortal, for according to a tenth-century writer, the monster was 'repulsive, outlandish, fierce and very terrifying.' It had a front end like a horse, two 'hideous thick legs' with 'iron claws' which 'struck showers of fire from the stony rocks' and a 'fiery breath which burned like embers.'

Armed with the Word of God, Senan ordered this dragon (if it was a dragon) to leave the island. Some versions of the story say that it left at once, running to Doo Lough Mount Callan. Another version says that the Cathaig fought, eating a blacksmith called Narach, so St Senan had to bring him back, still alive. Senan used the next weapon in his armoury, the sign of the Cross, which overpowered the Cathaig's resistance. Chaining it up, St Senan threw the beast in Doo Lough. That was not quite the end of the story, for the local king, or perhaps only a minor chieftain, took offence at the presence of the saint and asked a druid to put a curse on him. Naturally, in any contest between a saint and a druid, the saint will win, so when the druid stepped onto a small tidal island, the sea rose and swept him away.

That small island is still known as Carraig a Draoi, the Druid's Rock but there seems to be no more record of the dragon. However, if you are ever at the Doo Lough, I would be careful about swimming too far underwater.

TWENTY-FIVE

THE MOST HAUNTED CASTLE IN IRELAND

`

ALTHOUGH THIS CHAPTER INCLUDES GHOSTS, it is about a castle which undoubtedly deserves a place of its own. Leap Castle at Coolderry, County Offaly is often considered to be the most haunted castle in Ireland. If that is true, then Leap Castle must be fairly packed with ghosts. Because it is privately owned, nobody should visit Leap without the owner's express permission: even ghostly castles deserve privacy and Leap is no exception. I have read about, visited and written about many haunted and spooky castles. I had thought that Edinburgh or Glamis in Scotland topped my list, but Leap is in a league of its own. I have never come across such a collection of malignant people as those who lived here in the bad old days. There are several reasons why Leap should attract adverse publicity.

Leap is said to be on a crossing of ley-lines, which some people think helps produce the castle's sometimes sinister atmosphere. The castle was also built using stones from centuries-old hill-forts, a fact that is said to have disturbed the local people as such places were believed to be the home of the Sidh. Thirdly, Leap could be on a Druidical site. Certainly, the Druids seem to have been active in this area, but were they an unpleasant people? Would they give the castle the uncanny atmosphere that some have claimed to experience? Or are the Druids being blamed for the actions of some older and far more bloody religious group? Strange Jack does not know the answers: he can only ask the question, write down a few of the supposed spiritual happenings and allow people to make up their own minds.

Leap sits within a small valley in County Offaly, between Birr in Offaly and Roscrea in Tipperary. It has a very strategic location, guarding a pass through the Slieve Bloom Mountains that is a route between the coast and the Offaly Plain. The O'Carroll clan, which survived for around fifteen hundred years, was one of the early owners. The castle history and legends tell of numerous murders, poisons, sexual assaults and tortures within these ancient walls, so it is not surprising that many unhappy ghosts are roaming around. According to one legend, the O'Bannon clan, which was a sept of the O'Carrolls, built the original castle. At one point, two brothers disagreed who was to be the chieftain of the clan. In such cases, the strongest and best would be the chieftain, so they decided to leap off the rock where they wished to build the castle. If either of them survived, he would be chieftain. They jumped; one died, and the other built Leap Castle.

The ghosts of the castle include Tadhg Coach O'Carroll, the Wild Captain Darby and the Red Lady, with many more.

We'll have a look at Tadhg first. He was a supremely unpleasant fellow, was Tadhg, or One-Eyed Tadhg as he was known. He lived in the sixteenth century, a time when first Henry VIII and then Elizabeth of England sent armies across the sea to conquer Ireland. The presence of these invaders made the island a nightmare of war, massacres, rapine, torment and pure horror. People living under such conditions tend to either become cowed and docile or react with similar violence; the Irish are not by nature inclined to docility. The conditions created men such as Tadhg.

On one occasion, an army of English supporters under one Edmund Fahy advanced on Leap Castle. Tadhg defeated them and, according to legend, thrust the survivors into underground tunnels where they wandered, lost in the dark until they starved to death. Edmund Fahy's men can still be heard, moaning deep underground as they searched for release.

It may be the same Tadhg who committed fratricide. Tadhg and Thaddeus were brothers, and when their father, Mulrooney O'Carroll, died in 1532, they argued about who should be the chief. Thaddeus was a priest, which would have been a strange choice to lead such a warlike clan, but Tadhg was taking no chances. Waiting until Thaddeus was celebrating mass in the castle chapel, Tadhg murdered him, to become the undisputed chief. According to legend, Tadhg still waits beside the altar, ready to cut the throat of any visitor and drink their blood. Not surprisingly, the chapel became known as the Bloody Chapel, with the ghost of the priest still seen inside, as well in the stair below. There is also a light visible at the window of the chapel, shining across the valley, even when the chapel is unoccupied.

It was not the English who finally disposed of the formidable Tadhg but his cousin Calvagh O' Carroll, who murdered him in 1553. If the Irish had been able to combine their forces rather than indulging in clan and family feuds, it is unlikely that anybody would have defeated them.

Not content with murdering each other and sundry pro-English clansmen, the O'Carrolls also killed off friendly warriors. The story is a little hard to unravel but it appears that the McMahons were allies of the O'Carrolls, or perhaps they shared common enemies, or the McMahons might have merely been mercenaries. On one occasion in 1599, the McMahons defeated the Earl of Tyrone, one of their mutual adversaries in battle, after which the O'Carrolls invited the clan leaders to a feast at Leap. The McMahons attended quite happily, only for the O'Carrolls to poison the lot. It is perhaps understandable that the McMahons should now haunt the great hall.

It is also fitting that the O'Carroll's rule by fear and violence should be the cause of their downfall. In the seventeenth century, the O'Carroll's grabbed an Englishman named Captain Darby. It is unknown if Darby was a handsome man, but he seems to have been attractive in some way, for the daughter of the O'Carroll chieftain fell in love with him. After keeping Darby alive with regular supplies of food, the young lady decided to help him escape. Avoiding the guards, she unlocked Darby's dungeon door, and the two crept through the darkened castle. They nearly escaped without being seen, but the girl's brother found them on the stairs, drew his sword and attacked at once. Either the girl brought a weapon for the prisoner, or he picked one up elsewhere, for Darby drew his sword and killed O'Carroll.

Now that she was heir to the castle, the young woman married Captain Darby, and the two lived in the castle. Darby may not have been an O'Carroll, but he was no angel and soon earned the nickname of the Wild Captain. Naturally, this man managed to find treasure and hide it in Leap Castle. The Wild Captain had a chequered life, with the authorities throwing him into jail for treason. His sentence was long and solitary confinement in a Dublin dungeon is not conducive to rational thought so when Derby returned to

Leap, he had forgotten where he hid his fortune. Even to this day, his ghost can be seen hunting for the wealth that fate took away from him.

Naturally, there is another version of the Wild Captain story, which goes something like this: Captain Jonathan Darby was a soldier of Cromwell's army. In 1649 the then government that controlled Ireland handed him Leap Castle because of his efforts to subdue the Irish. While at Leap, his wife, Deborah, gave birth to a son who was also named Jonathan. It was this second Jonathan who earned the sobriquet of Wild Captain Darby. Unlike his father, he was a royalist; like his father, he was a man of ambition. The Wild Captain was not a pleasant man. Marrying a local O'Carroll lady, he seized her lands around the Slieve Bloom mountains and treated her like dirt. He ground his tenants underfoot, beat his servants and invited his equally unsavoury friends for parties of drunken debauchery at Leap Castle.

The Wild Captain was reputed to have amassed a fortune in gold and jewellery. Nobody seems quite sure from where he obtained this treasure, but if it existed at all, the Wild Captain would not have garnered it by quiet labour. According to the story, this Wild Captain created a secret chamber within the walls of Leap and forced two of his servants to carry his treasure there. With the wealth in place, the Wild Captain casually murdered the servants, before bricking corpses and treasure in the castle. In 1693 Wild Jonathan married Anna Maria d'Esterre, and five years later he was arrested for treason. Sentenced to be hanged, drawn and quartered, he languished within his damp dungeon in Dublin, waiting for that horrible death.

However, King William, he of the Orange hue, pardoned him and Wild Jonathan returned to his castle, but not the same man. Imprisonment and the prospect of imminent execution had unhinged his mind. He could not even remember where he had hidden his treasure. It may be still there, hidden somewhere in Leap Castle. Unfortunate people can still meet the Wild Captain on certain days, as he wanders the grounds searching for the treasure he lost. Well, it serves him right for being a murdering hound.

Whichever version of the Wild Captain legend one prefers, he seems to have been a nasty man.

Possibly the saddest ghost at Leap is the Red Lady, who is tall and apparently very beautiful. Beauty can sometimes be a curse in itself, for one of the O'Carrolls saw the Red Lady and immediately fell for her. He captured the lady, dragged her to Leap and imprisoned her, after which he raped her, not once but many times. When the lady eventually gave birth to her captor's child, the evil O'Carroll murdered the baby with the excuse that he could not afford to feed it. Unable to stand her grief, the Red Lady killed herself. Now she haunts the Blue Room, which was once the nursery, dressed in scarlet silk and holding the knife with which she committed suicide. Some people have seen her surrounded by a strange light, while others have said she had a fire around her head or that they felt a chill emanating from her.

Leap had the cheek to have its private chapel, presumably so the inhabitants could ask forgiveness from God for the murders and horrors that they inflicted on their neighbours and any others unfortunate enough to cross their path. However, even the chapel had its secrets. In this case, one of the walls hid an oubliette, which is a dungeon with only one means of access, a hole at the top through which the jailors lowered prisoners on the end of a rope. Of course, sometimes the residents of the castle were less kind and threw the prisoners bodily through the hatch. That seems to be what happened at Castle Leap, for when people discovered the oubliette, they found if full of skeletons impaled on spikes. If that were true, then the O'Carrolls dropped their prisoners onto spikes set in the oubliette floor. Vlad the Impaler would have been proud of this castle although some kind historian has suggested that this little chamber was only a mediaeval safe, a storage place for the castle's treasures. The name oubliette is French 'to forget.' When it was rediscovered, three wagons were needed to cart away the bones, or so it is claimed.

Perhaps there is something in the fabric of Leap Castle that attracts spirits, or maybe the castle was indeed built on the site of some ancient disturbance, for a much later Darby left her mark on this haunted place. When she was not writing gothic novels, Mildred Darby held séances in Leap. People blame her for stirring some dark force within the castle, to add to the already busy spiritual presence. This entity is said to be either a long-dead O'Carroll with leprosy or something very much older and worse. This thing either looks tall and gaunt or is about four feet high with burning holes where its eyes should be. Whatever or whoever it is, there is no doubt that one is advised to avoid it.

In 1922 the Darbys finally left Leap. As so often, Ireland was in turmoil with another war against British rule. Despite their centuries in Ireland, the Darbys regarded themselves as English rather than Irish. The empty castle with British links became a target for the Irish Republican Army, who bombed it and decorated the tower by hanging the resident peacocks from meat hooks or possibly crucifying them, for reasons of their own. For more than half a century, Leap lay empty until the 1970s when Peter Bartlett, an Australian historian whose distant ancestors were the O'Bannons, who founded the place, moved in. During Bartlett's fifteen years in restoring the castle, he experienced a great deal of poltergeist movement, so asked a white witch to remove the unwanted spirits. The witch reported that the spirits remained, but promised not to cause any problems. The next owner was a musician named Sean Ryan, who continued the restoration, despite constant poltergeist activity and a spate of injuries.

The castle remains haunted. People have heard the moans of Edmund Fahy's soldiers under the ground. Sometimes people hear children crying deep inside the castle. There is the ghost of a tall woman clad in red, with her hand raised and what appears to be a fire around her head. There is also a phantom monk wandering the corridors, footsteps with no visible presence and, outside the walls, a man in a long cloak lurks. Added to that is an elderly man in knee breeches, buckled shoes and a green coat, who sounds more like a leprechaun than a spirit. This green gentleman sometimes carries a leather bag, like a doctor, and occasionally has a female companion with a large head dress and black gloves that extend up her arms. The man in green can be seen trying to talk to people, and sometimes has another companion, dressed as a priest but with a devious face. The front doorbell has rung without anybody being there, and there is the sound of chanting.

Added to that is the mysterious Muckle-hole or Murder Room, which had a stain on the floor where a man had been murdered. Although the stain has been scrubbed and planed off, it still returns, according to the story. Is that not enough for any reasonably haunted castle? Well, it's not sufficient for Leap, for there is more.

There is a roughly dressed man, who pushes a barrel up the back stairs until he nears the top, when the barrel clatters down the stairs again, giving him an eternity of physical labour. The main hall has two young girls who scamper up the stairs, dressed in the fashion of the early seventeenth century. One of these youngsters may be Emily, who was eleven when she fell from the battlements at the south-east of the castle. . Her companion may be named Charlotte, a girl who was known to be lame in one leg. There are occasions when people see the girls with an older lady, known in the castle as the Nanny or the Governess, and she wears Victorian clothes, so ghosts from hundreds of years apart gather together in this spirit-friendly place. The Priest's House has a visiting monk, who enters by one window and leaves by another, silent and harmless.

The list continues as if every generation who has lived here added its quota of spirits. I have not yet mentioned the half-naked woman who screams through the red cloth that covers her face and then vanishes, leaving a sensation of intense cold, or the two O'Carroll brothers who are said to be fighting over a woman for eternity. Overall, Leap Castle is undoubtedly unique in the number and variety of ghosts it has. If anywhere in Ireland deserves the title of 'most haunted,' it is Leap.

TWENTY-SIX
THE HELLFIRE CLUB

THE NAME GIVES A CLUE. Any club that advertises itself as hell is probably not intended for church-goers or innocent pastimes of flower-arranging, and eighteenth-century Dublin's Hellfire Club was no exception. The name is commonly applied to a building on Mount Pelier, a 1257-foot-high hill in County Dublin. The club itself operated from 1735 to 1741, and then again from 1771 until the turn of the eighteenth and nineteenth centuries.

The building that became known as the Hellfire Club, and where the members gathered, was originally a hunting lodge for William Connolly, a Speaker of the Irish House of Commons, in 1725. He bought it from Philip, the Duke of Wharton who had founded the English Hell Fire Club. The place is also known as Montpelier House and sits at Kilakee in the Dublin Mountains. Connolly laid the foundations for horror, for he chose a site where there was a Neolithic passage grave topped with a cairn. Destroying the cairn, Connolly retained a standing stone to use as the lintel for his fireplace, thus annoying the spirits, Sidh, or whatever, that inhabited the place. Locals shook their head, saying that no good would come of such blasphemy, and within months they were proved right when a sudden gale blasted the roof clean off. Unfazed, Connolly rebuilt the roof with a natty arch, still using stones from the burial cairn.

As if a politician was not bad enough, when Connolly died, four years later, his widow did not know what to do with the building, so eventually rented it out to an unpleasant, drunken man who moved in after every pub in Dublin had barred him. Having been in some of Dublin's finest, I can affirm that it must take some notoriety for every pub in the city to bar anybody. Such a man must attract trouble, and when he invited his friends, young men of similar habits, the house became a centre of wild excesses. The new lease-holder was said to be Richard Parsons, the Earl of Rosse, who helped found the Young Bucks of Dublin, otherwise known as the Dublin branch of the Hellfire Club. As the name 'Bucks' implies, these were all 'gentlemen', which is a somewhat elastic term that meant they had position, but the evidence suggests they had no morals. Indeed, Jonathan Swift called them 'monsters, blasphemers and Bacchanalians.' Parsons' reputation included worse things than mere drunkenness; he was said to practice black magic at a time that fear of witchcraft was very much alive. He also had the habit of inviting people to his home and greeting them entirely naked, which could either have been disconcerting or highly amusing, depending on the guest's point of view. When the visitor was a clergyman, perhaps Rosse was more amused than his guest.

Other members were rumoured to do worse than childish practical jokes. In the second incarnation of the club, Thomas 'Buck' Whaley was said to have led the members in murdering and then eating a young girl.

The Hellfire Club became known for immorality and drunkenness, with dark whispers of Satan worship that the members probably encouraged to keep outsiders away. According to the stories, the club's president was called 'The King of Hell' and dressed the part, while every time they met; the members left a space in case the devil decided to join them. On one occasion, he did just that, sliding in to play cards and vanishing in a ball of flame when one of the members noticed his hooves. Only slightly less outlandish is the legend that the club sacrificed cats and servants during their black masses.

There are so many wild stories that I suspect the members made them up themselves. For instance, there was a member caught cheating at cards, so the other members tied him up, thrust him into a hogshead of whiskey and burned him alive. I don't believe that men known for their heavy drinking would waste whiskey in that manner. Much more likely is the tradition that the members had a special drink called scaltheen, which was a mixture of whiskey and hot butter.

One story says that a local farmer joined the club one night to see what happened, but was so afraid, he lost his memory and power of speech. There was also the tall tale of a servant spilling Whaley's drink, only for Whaley to burn the man alive, and the story that the members sacrificed a dwarf one day. Whatever the truth and however much the stories have grown in the telling, even professional ghost hunters have been scared by the atmosphere at the ruin known as the Hellfire Club, which is said to be one of the creepiest places in Ireland. Casual visitors have reported feeling their chest tighten and a strange sensation in their head, so the nervous or overly susceptible are advised not to visit. There is even a tale that one woman brought something ugly back with her, something that followed her home, so she continued to hear its footsteps, night after night. Others who visit the site have spoken of a variety of ugly things from a black shadow that passes them to seeing a ghostly black cat the size of a dog, with blazing eyes and pointed ears. (Don't all cats have pointed ears?) That tale may have evolved from the legend that a priest visited the Hellfire Club and found the members sacrificing a black cat. He interfered with an exorcism that saw a demon burst free of the cat's dead body. Another version claims the priest sprinkled holy water on the cat, which turned into a demon.

Other people have heard voices whispering 'get out', while people walking on the hill have felt invisible hands snatch at their crucifixes. And that is without mentioning that the members once thrust a woman inside a barrel, which was set alight and pushed down the hill.

If you are only on a short visit to Ireland and wish to experience the strangest of places, then the Hellfire Club would be the perfect place to see. I have only to give the obvious advice that you should be very prepared to experience anything before you go, and take great care when you get there. Some things are best left alone.

L'ENVOI

So that is my take on Strange Ireland. It is an island of tradition and open-hearted welcomes, a tragic history and hopefully a bright future. For every story included, I have left out a hundred. Ireland is an island of ready wit, a green land whose smile hides a hundred thousand tales, of which this little book has introduced only a handful. It would take a woman or a man a lifetime to learn them all, and by the time he or she finished, there would be three score years plus ten more of legend, mythology and mystery to add to the total.

I carried back from Ireland a thousand legends and sufficient memories to fill another book. I remember the sideways slant of Monica's eyes as she told me another ghost story, the vast bleakness of the Burren, the atmosphere of Tara, the drift of music in a Dublin pub, the call of birds that sounded so much like a Banshee that the hairs on the nape of my neck lifted. But most of all, perhaps, I remembered that single hawthorn tree on a Belfast golf course and the laughter in a man's voice as I asked him about any strange events in county Clare.

'Strange events?' He said. 'There's nothing that happens here that isn't strange.'

Having travelled the length and breadth of the island, I can accept his wisdom. Ireland is a never-ending pot of strangeness, and long may that continue.

Jack Strange

Dublin and Moray, Spring 2019

Printed in Poland
by Amazon Fulfillment
Poland Sp. z o.o., Wrocław